A Bite-Sized Public Affairs Book

The Generation Game

Can the BBC win over today's young audience?

**Edited by
Michael Wilson
and Neil Fowler**

Cover by
Dean Stockton

Published by Bite-Sized Books Ltd 2020
©Michael Wilson and Neil Fowler 2020

Bite-Sized Books Ltd Cleeve Road, Goring RG8 9BJ UK
information@bite-sizedbooks.com
**Registered in the UK. Company Registration
No: 9395379**

ISBN: 9798665954899

Contents

Sound bites

Vox Populi

Acknowledgements

On April 3, two weeks into my own Covid-19 lockdown, and then subsequent self-isolation, I read the Bite-Sized Book *Is the BBC in Peril? Does it Deserve to Be?,* edited by John Mair and Tom Bradshaw.

It's a superb collection of essays around the politics, both internal and external, the pressures of journalism and bias, the threats, the opportunities and the unique place the BBC holds in British culture.

I had written for a couple of the editors' other books and emailed to both John and Paul Davies, the publisher at Bite-Sized Books, suggesting one area to further the debate was why young people are not tuning into the BBC.

Ofcom, the Government and the BBC itself have seen this as a major issue. As a result Paul encouraged the project which has become this book – published only three months later in July 2020.

My thanks to John and Tom for being the catalysts, Paul for having faith in this project as my first outing as an editor, and his guidance always positive through the process.

A huge thank you to co-editor Neil Fowler whose knowledge of media and journalism issues, ability to craft superb commentary and endless patience have made delivering *The Generation Game* (indeed the title is his!) against tight deadlines achievable and even enjoyable.

Thanks to Dean Stockton – for his inspirational cover design.

Thank you also to all the countless agents, media officers, colleagues and friends who made introductions, forwarded emails and shared contacts to get to the cast of contributors.

The deepest thanks have to go to all the contributors who have given their words and thoughts and insights. They excelled in delivering on the brief – without any payment – during the height of the Covid-19 crisis. Their pressure from work and family must have been amplified many times more than normal and yet still they have been able to contribute. I stand and applaud you all.

Collectively you have made a significant addition to the debate on one of the core issues for the future survival of the BBC.

And finally…this book is dedicated to my family:

To Mum and Dad and Sally for always being there – sorry since lockdown I haven't been!

To Deborah - you never cease to amaze me. For your endless support and ideas, and for putting up with my 'projects' like trying to turn around a book in 10 weeks. I love you.

And especially to Teddy. When he asks in years to come, "What did you do during lockdown Daddy?", I can show him this volume and he can decide if it was time well spent!

Michael Wilson

The editors

Michael Wilson is an experienced chief executive, managing director, board member and editor-in-chief with more than 30 years' business and leadership experience in the content creation, broadcasting, media, communications and digital sectors. He has held senior roles at national and international level including Sky News, Five News, UTV Northern Ireland and ITV.

He now runs a consultancy business specialising in content and platform strategy specifically working with the boards and C-levels leaders of major international businesses. He is also the CEO of the Isle of Media, the national development agency for the Isle of Man digital and creative industries. For more than a decade he was managing director of the ITV region in Northern Ireland – UTV - and represented UTV on the board of ITV Network. He is Managing Director of fine art business Paul Yates Art, and an Entrepreneur in Residence at Catalyst, the Northern Ireland Science Park.

He sits on the Royal Television Society's Centre's council and is a founder member of the Irish Film and Television Academy. His programming has won Baftas, RTS's awards and New York Television Festival Awards. He's a published contributing author, media and business commentator and currently lives in Switzerland.

Neil Fowler has been in journalism since graduation, starting life as trainee reporter on the Leicester Mercury. He went on to edit four regional dailies, including *The Journal* in the north east of England and *The Western Mail* in Wales. He was then publisher of *The Toronto Sun* in Canada before returning to the UK to edit *Which?* magazine.

In 2010/11 he was the Guardian Research Fellow at Oxford University's Nuffield College where he investigated the decline and future of regional and local newspapers in the UK. From then until 2016 he helped organise the college's prestigious David Butler media and politics seminars. As well as being an occasional contributor to trade magazines he now acts as an adviser to organisations on their management and their external and internal communications and media policies and strategies.

Foreword

Reading for the new DG

Michael Wilson

The BBC has a critical problem – and it is the focus of all levels of the corporation. Young people are not tuning into its television and radio. There is panic at the top of the organisation. What will the future hold for the backbone of British broadcasting? How will the licence fee be justified? New technology is sucking away eyeballs and the young audience is finding new forms of electronic entertainment.

That's not 2020, but it was the case in 1990.

Sky's multi-channel offering was gaining traction after launching a couple of years earlier; gaming consoles were *de rigueur*; and the BBC was battling by bringing in Janet Street-Porter – fresh from her success in commercial broadcasting – to steady the ship and to launch new programmes aimed at keeping the next generation of viewers. The BBC was on a war footing to win the 'yoof audience'.

It was about this time I started my career in broadcasting. During my years at university I spent more hours in the offices of the BBC in Nottingham than I did on the campus in lectures. And while at university I was producing the weekly 'youth' output across four radio stations in the East Midlands. The programme name changed a few times, but became *The Beat* and was presented by a teacher with the radio-bug called Dean Jackson.

Today 30 years later that programme still exists and has the same presenter. We must have done something right back then!

I remember when the film *Dances with Wolves* was released. A major film, a major star in Kevin Costner and *The Beat* had a major interview and a prize give away.

For the show it was huge, so the week after the competition aired we had picked a winner, picked out from hundreds of postcards placed into a hat – long before text or email entries – and we sent the radio car off with an entertainment reporter to personally hand over this prize package to the winner in Nottingham's suburbia.

This was all a surprise of course; trying to build a little drama on air. The reporter rigged the car, ran the cables to the winner's door and rang the bell. We waited, and waited, all live on air – in broadcasting even 10 seconds can seem a lifetime – but the door eventually opened.

The winner of the competition on the supposed young people's output was a pensioner, propped on a Zimmer frame, and looking slightly startled at the small media circus at their front door.

Years later, the ITV regional company of which I was managing director had just launched a radio station for those closer to middle age than school age, and our business editor complained to me that the station was playing the wrong music. He was close to retirement and said the music was far too old for the demographic – he was buying artists far more chart-orientated than the station's playlist.

The point of both stories is its close to impossible to pigeon hole content for tight demographics, as inevitably there is cross over. More importantly, good content reaches all audiences.

Fleabag and *Normal People* are watched by all ages; the graph doesn't just flatline at 30 because they were commissioned with a younger demographic in mind.

I remember being around the table of the grandly named ITV Council, the board of ITV Network, and the holy grail of young eyeballs was discussed regularly.

Often of major interest to the advertising agencies, ITV needed to stay young to keep the revenue coming in. Again, when asked what programmes brought in the largest young audience, it wasn't the shows commissioned especially for young people, but programmes like *Coronation Street*, *Emmerdale* and *The X-Factor*. These huge audience juggernauts deliver large volumes across all demographics.

It will be the same with the BBC – drama successes such as *Peaky Blinders*, soaps like *EastEnders* and entertainment like *Strictly* will deliver more young people, both on linear and digital than niche content aimed for their eyes only.

While researching this book one contributor Alex DeGroote told me his sons love *Dad's Army* and share YouTube clips with their friends – great BBC content, but the kids don't relate it to being delivered or produced by the BBC.

So why this book, and why now?

Four reasons:

Firstly, the BBC half-term report is planned in a year or so. Under the current Royal Charter a review is prescribed in 2022. The BBC, the Government and Ofcom have all said the delivery of young eyeballs and ears is key to the sustainability of the licence fee as a funding mechanism long term. While there is no real alternative funding option, if you wish to have a BBC of the scale and scope we have now, the review will most likely give a clear indication of the routes favoured at the next Charter renewal.

Secondly, the Covid-19 crisis has seen the attention and criticism being turned down regarding the BBC. Many regard the BBC as being the nation's voice at times of crisis and, indeed, young people have tuned in in numbers not seen for many years. Behind that, however, has been a huge increase in subscriptions to the likes of Netflix and when normality returns (whatever that looks like), the BBC may actually be in a weaker position.

The third reason is the news in the latest BBC annual plan that the future of BBC Three is being debated (again). Lost as a linear channel, it became an online service and now it's a kind of hybrid with a presence on BBC One and online. The timing seems right to look at the best way forward in detail. With new Director-General Tim Davie taking the corner office in September, the ideas in this book, may make a suitable addition to add to his reading list. I will certainly be sending him a copy.

And finally, and perhaps most importantly, having worked in broadcasting for more than three decades I have never actually seen a real debate on what works when programming content for a young audience.

My honest view is audience segmentation is at best a mystical art and successes are often luck rather than judgement. A well-made popular programme such as *Blue Planet* derives as much kudos with a young audience as content aimed directly at them. Indeed the (very unscientific) vox pops, with a selection of young people, all mention mainstream shows being why they watch the BBC – rather than niche content.

This book hopefully focuses on the hard actions needed to win back the young audience. It's not just about the programming, but a wide range of issues and challenges that a multi-platform, multi-device and multi-cultural environ-ment has thrown up.

Introduction

Let the sun shine on the lost generation

Mike Read offers hope for the BBC – but says passion and a willingness to go outside corporate norms is required

So Ofcom has shown the BBC a yellow card and warned that it should be winning back younger viewers. To that end it has wheeled out Gertrude Stein's phrase, popularised by Hemingway – *The Lost Generation.*

How delightfully dramatic. It's a series in itself as 20 to 30-year-olds are specifically mentioned, flagging up our obsession with dividing all aspects of life into neat, decade-long chunks. If younger audiences are drifting away from the BBC, they must be drifting away from all mainstream television, not just the BBC.

The corporation is not in competition with other channels; it is there to provide a service at many levels.

It has always covered a wide range of genres including news, history, entertainment, arts, politics, sport and more, through ten national TV channels, regional programmes and an internet service as well as ten national radio stations, 40 local radio stations and the BBC World Service, with news and information in some 40 languages.

It offers a veritable plethora of choices across a wide range of platforms. Does Ofcom know what the 20-30s would like for the BBC to woo them back, if anything?

A 24-year-old can enjoy the same football match as a 68-year-old. They can both participate in the same quiz shows. They can both be interested in *Question Time.* They can both be passionate about documentaries. Is the Ofcom question a veiled hint that maybe the BBC should be dumbing down for the younger viewer?

Younger people may simply not be as interested in television as they were. These things happen. Lifestyles change. In the 1980s *Top of the Pops* was getting a regular audience of some 15m, but no-one thought creatively enough and it was eventually eased into Room 101.

I could see what it should have done and to that end offered to take it over free for a year to turn it around. My offer was rejected.

Was that in case it might just work and reveal shortcomings in letting it slide so far down the ratings? Even on *Saturday Superstore* and *Pop Quiz* we were getting around the 10m mark every week for both shows.

More choice

Now, of course, there's more choice. Young people are appreciative of music but maybe not so committed or so passionate. Streaming has made everything more accessible, more instant and more manoeuvrable, while the BBC is perceived as an impenetrable pantechnicon, struggling to find a suitable parking space. Is Ofcom asking it to pursue the unpursuable?

Going into Broadcasting House every day I was reminded of the Reithian principles: 'Inform-Educate-Entertain', but now, pushed by political agendas and Ofcom to achieve higher performance levels, it should surely be amended to '*Citius-*

Altius-Fortius'- faster, higher, stronger. The answer to 'we must cater more for the younger viewers,' is usually met by bringing in younger decision makers as they allegedly know what the young want.

Partially maybe, but younger people have such diverse interests now and being in a certain age bracket doesn't necessarily mean you have the finger on the pulse of your own generation. A media-trained male Londoner of 27 may be poles apart from the televisual wants and needs of a female of the same age in another part of the country.

A tricky dilemma

The BBC, it seems, is allowed neither to win nor to lose. A tricky dilemma for any business.

The idea of a television streaming service for the BBC was mooted back in 2007 at the time of the launch of the iPlayer. The service would have included Hollywood movies and content from not only the corporation but also ITV and Channel 4. A forward-looking idea that would have continued to keep younger viewers engaged.

It was to be the best of British TV and popular films with three major channels working together. The service was to be a prototype Britbox named Kangaroo. The system was on the starting block and ready to go when it was referred by the Office of Fair Trading to the government's Competition Commission.

A non-media and non-technical panel blocked the venture deeming it to be too much of a threat to competition in a developing market.

I believe the BBC worked best when it was a smaller organisation, with different departments supporting each other and working together to achieve great results. It seemed to me to become gradually more compartmentalised.

When I first presented the breakfast show from Wimbledon I was able to use the archive, source and use the audio of historic matches and integrate them into my programme. Later we were asked for a fee to source them and an even bigger fee for usage. *Ergo*, I had to stop using them, disappointing both our listeners and the current players I was interviewing.

I am pressured constantly on social media to ask the BBC to re-run the 50 or so *Pop Quiz* programmes. I have asked on several occasions, but there they remain in the archive until they escape one by one from substandard video copies onto YouTube for which no-one gets paid.

Now Ofcom is asking why the BBC isn't up to speed and is losing younger audiences. Knee-jerk reaction isn't the answer and there is also the very real danger that older viewers would be lost as the BBC falls between those these target groups.

To that end I would temporarily replace 'Inform-Educate-Entertain' with '*Non cadunt inter duas scholas*' – do not fall between two stools. If the BBC TV were to attempt to win back younger audiences it should look to bring in people who have passion, who inspire, who have creative thoughts and not those happy to be restricted by the company parameters while taking the King's shilling.

Ofcom warns that, by its centenary, the sun may have set on the BBC thanks to 'The Lost Generation.' So let the corporation take heart from the title of the novel that popularised the phrase....*The Sun Also Rises*.

About the writer

Mike Read has been a broadcaster for more than 40 years, hosting various radio shows for the BBC as well as presenting television programmes such as *Top of the Pops*, *Saturday Superstore* and *Pop Quiz*. He has won many awards for broadcasting, song writing and as an author. Mike has had forty books published, was created a Knight of Malta in 2011 and is Chairman of the British Plaque Trust.

Vox Populi

Phoebe Powers, 19, student, Wigan

The BBC feels formal and serious.

I do watch BBC news and use the iPlayer – it's great to have a service that doesn't have adverts.

I think a lot of the content I watch is entertaining, but I would watch and consume more if there were more programmes for young people.

Chapter 1

Reaching kids is hard, but somehow harder for the BBC

Every traditional broadcaster is struggling with audience decline, especially the young, and the BBC is doing worse than its commercial rivals. There are structural reasons for this, but instead of moaning, bold moves should be made to address what is an existential problem for the broadcaster, writes Tom Harrington

For traditional television broadcasters reaching viewers has never been harder. While in 2010 an individual watched an average four hours and two minutes of broadcast television (live and catchup) every day, by 2019 it was three hours and three minutes.

These averages are held up to a great extent by the very oldest in society: 97-year-olds, for example, still watch a six hours and 20 minutes per day (lucky them!), with those below the age of about 45 declining more than the overall average.

While older viewers are holding on, generally the younger the demographic, the greater the decline. In 2019, for example, viewing by 16-24-year-olds was just 41 per cent of 2010 levels (those over 65 stayed almost stable over the same period).

It is a tough environment for all traditional broadcasters. However, in terms of reaching young viewers, the BBC has done worse than its commercial competitors: weekly reach for its family of channels has dropped since 2010 from 82 per cent (for 4-15s and 16-34s) to 58 per cent (4-15s) and 60 per cent (16-34s), respectively.

Commercial television has seen the smaller decline in reach of 89 per cent to 79 per cent, and 88 per cent to 79 per cent for those two demographics.

What does this mean for daily use? Whereas in 2010 those aged 4-15 watched 42 minutes of BBC programming per day, in 2019 they watched only 17 minutes, while for 16-34s the drop was from 47 minutes to just under 20. (Note: the Covid-19-inflicted lockdown gave a temporary, but unsurprising bump to all the quoted figures.)

So why is youth viewing falling faster than that of older viewers? Where is their attention going?

It may well be the case that the division in taste, politics and general interests are splitting generations to a greater extent than ever before. However, the fundamental dichotomy between the old and the young when it comes to television and video viewing is the growing availability of multiple devices in the home and the greater likelihood of the young using them.

Television sets are just as commonplace in the home as ever – for some time the number of households depriving themselves of television (at least on a proper screen) has hovered around 4 to 5 per cent. But whereas, in the past, the variety of entertainment options were few outside the living room set (likely to have been controlled by an older family member) phones and tablets give the younger consumer a myriad of options from which *they* get to choose.

And so, young people are not watching less video – in fact they are watching more, year-on-year – they are just watching it in different ways and from different outlets (for 16-34s, around 50 per cent of their video viewed comes from elsewhere than linear and catchup TV, compared to around 20 per cent for the over 55s).

Outside of the linear schedule the public service broadcasters (PSBs) are not afforded prominence, and other operators can negotiate for their service to be given prime real estate.

Nor do broadcast codes cover the content watched on YouTube (which we estimate those aged 4-15 watch on average 48 minutes per day, and those 16-34 even more) with much of what is watched and apparently interests the young, such as dumb violent pranks, 'social experiments' or questionable vlogging, not something that traditional television would be allowed to replicate.

Furthermore, as smart TVs or dongles have become standard and apps for YouTube and streaming services have become available on the biggest screen in the house, the viewing trends fortified on devices have moved to the TV set as well.

Why it is harder for the BBC?

All broadcasters have been challenged by this shift. Unlike streaming services such as Netflix or Amazon, which provide their subscribers with a library of content and then let them at it, there is a constant challenge for traditional broadcasters to address and split resources between two different types of viewing – the live linear schedule, which remains incredibly important to many, and online, on-demand viewing, which skews younger and is undoubtedly the future.

At other points in time when the BBC has been troubled by splits in its audience it has been in a stronger position.

Through the 1960s, for example, growth in television ownership drove increases in revenue from the licence fee. However recently, the BBC has found itself with less financial flexibility.

The BBC claimed £712m in sustainable (i.e. yearly, ongoing) savings were achieved during its Delivering Quality First initiative, which looked to cut 20 per cent of its cost base after the licence fee freeze and which finished in April 2017.

A savings programme, currently on hold due to the surge in Covid-19 news demand, will see up to 450 jobs cut, as the news service is restructured into story teams which will supply all outlets, in order to erase the inefficiency of multiple takes on the same matter.

The BBC stated that in 2018/19 it delivered £153m in efficiency savings. Current uncertainty over who should pay for the licences of the over 75s could end up with the BBC burdened further.

With revenue from the licence fee declining in real terms and the cost of content rising, there is only one outcome – cutting back on content spend, services and continued development of iPlayer (once best in class, but now lagging behind foreign streaming services in terms of user experience).

The ability to make the shows that it wants is hampered by cost inflation, meaning that projects move elsewhere or the BBC has a smaller stake and less control.

There is an unrelenting pressure to fill schedules, knowing that reruns or a drop in quality will accelerate the move towards streaming services. The terms of trade between the BBC and independent producers, which hand most of the rights (after the initial broadcast and catchup) of programme commissions back to the producer, has hamstrung the development of iPlayer into anything more than a catchup service, while the foreign streamers have the online space catering for browsing viewers all to themselves.

At the same time the BBC's major streaming rivals are either loss-making or debt-funded, with their massive content and tech expenditure not wholly reliant upon subscriber revenue, with price points set aggressively low due to the desire to quickly build scale within a nascent, competitive market.

These prices are perennially compared to the cost of the licence fee, which has implications for its perceived value. In this regard it is not a fair fight. The BBC can't borrow heavily due to regulations, optics and the essentially non-commercial nature of much of its output and research, not to mention the imprudence, and as such it must, generally, make do with progressively less.

Although many of the comparisons between the BBC and the streaming services are facile, and in regard to the argument that the BBC should be a subscription service, naïve of most of the complexities, in the mind of the consumer they are not.

How it could do better

Netflix and the BBC are both providers of television content, but the breadth of the BBC's slate (covering genres that Netflix never will, including news, current affairs, sport and national events, as well as providing radio services) and the remit, which it must fulfil to among other things drive UK production, regionality and representation on screen, are irrelevant.

 This perception of irrelevance is a problem. Although the user-generated content of YouTube has stolen youth engagement from the BBC, the likes of Netflix and Amazon are crucially not selling anything new – it is still television content. And for a long time (although this is rapidly diminishing) a lot of what has been watched has been the *same* content.

The terms of trade is partly responsible for this, as the BBC has no control as to where much of the content it commissions ends up after catchup.

For some time Netflix was the biggest customer of BBC Worldwide (now BBC Studios), the corporation's commercial distribution arm, selling BBC content to the streamer both internationally and domestically and allowing it to have a recognisable library of content during its nascency in the UK.

The BBC shouldn't be blamed for chasing cheques given its financial limitations, however this revenue stream was always going to be temporary given the trajectory of Netflix's original content investment, and this should have weighed more into the decision to deal with them (others have chosen not to).

Similarly, embarking on co-productions with Netflix (also clearly a temporary funding opportunity) may have made a few productions feasible that otherwise may not have been, but the transfer to the foreign company of local knowhow, production expertise and the opportunity to review and hire away competent staff may be a net loss.

And then BBC Three. Banished from linear television to behind a tab (behind another tab) on the iPlayer it has been no surprise that despite some excellent content (*This Country*, *Normal People*, *Pls Like*) it has, according to a new study, lost about 90 per cent of viewing, or around 75 per cent if broadcasts of BBC Three programming on BBC One and BBC Two are included.

It never had a massive audience. In 2016, prior to its axing from linear, it had a weekly reach amongst 16-34s of 28 per cent, but it was an identifiable brand and location for youth-targeted viewing. And it utilised one of the advantages of being a public service broadcaster – prominence on the linear schedule.

The BBC is now considering returning BBC Three to the linear world and, given its prominence (something that the BBC is unable to harness online and on smart TVs and platforms), at the very least it is a handy barker channel for iPlayer, advertising some of the full series available on the service, but hidden by its poor layout.

Current placement of BBC Three longform content sits incongruously after the *News at Ten* on BBC One. The mooted doubling of content budget will return it nearer to its former level (although still £20m less than its previous £80m) and, given that it shared its terrestrial bandwidth with CBBC (BBC Three only operated at night), there are transmission cost synergies that still remain.

The timing of all this?

Is it too late? Well, probably. But at the very least this is a bold move amongst a lot of dithering and defeatism. To this day there exists moaning about the then Competition Commission's blocking of Kangaroo – the pre-Netflix streaming service from the PSBs – even though it would have faced the same conceptual obstacles as the current iteration, BritBox, namely trying to sell content that people think (incorrectly, but relevantly) that they have already paid for.

Earlier this year the Danish Broadcasting Corporation – the BBC equivalent in a country with an even more rapid viewing decline among the young – moved its youth channels DR3 and DR Ultra online. RTÉ's youth channel is rumoured to be going the same way. But these moves are not based on what is best but what is cheapest, and with the problem around youth viewing undoubtedly an existential one for the BBC, it would be suicide to be frugal.

About the writer

Tom Harrington is a senior analyst at Enders Analysis, the UK's leading TMT research company. He is regularly quoted in major publications and interviewed on radio and television. He has degrees from Sydney and Cambridge.

Sound bite #1

Anthea Turner, presenter, *Top of the Pops*, 1988-91; *Blue Peter* 1992-94

How did the BBC generally lose the young audience they held so dear? I have to liken it to Kodak, Blockbuster and the Hackney Carriage Company: all were asleep at the wheel and for some unknown reason, despite tsunami-type tremors and warnings, it didn't see it coming.

The BBC had my generation in the palms of its hands. Brian Cant on Play School *taught me to swim without water over a kitchen stool;* Blue Peter *made me part of their family; I shared their pets, their holidays, adventures, cooked, made things and supported their charities.*

Saturday-morning TV was the FOMO of its day, so nothing got done until it was over; sitting in Stoke on Trent, Top of the Pops *was my window on all things trendy.*

Most of us who were part of that generation are still staunch supporters of the BBC. Our default button, especially for major events, is BBC news – nothing else we believe or satisfies us.

Other contributors who know better than I in this book will take you through the demise of children's programming; how the industry has changed in tandem with the requirements of the young; and how many great brains have scratched their heads over this subject and tried a myriad of approaches.

I am going to make two points one business and one emotional:

* *The BBC, for some reason, never saw its programmes as brands growing – marketing and developing the programmes by not only appealing to new generations*

but subtly integrating themselves into young lives outside of a television programme. Why isn't Blue Peter, for instance, a benchmark for excellence in education, setting up school initiatives, awards – and the same for Newsround, *which the BBC recently got rid of and allowed a new kid on the block (Sky's* FYI*) to scoop trophies, proving kids still want their own news programme.*

- *Never lose the emotion of belonging. Banks and other commercial institutions understand this, which is why these companies spend so much time and money cultivating the young.*

Have they gone never to return? I don't think so and my reason is the Blue Planet *generation.*

They are captivated and emotionally invested by this juggernaut of truth and want to be part of the solution. Draw them in and make them feel they are invested in an environmental movement spearheaded by the BBC.

We are all fully paid-up members of Hindsight Productions and for its faults and mistakes the BBC is a truly amazing organisation. It is a standard bearer for broadcasting. It is ours and we should do everything in our power to hold it dear and never let it go.

Chapter 2

OK, Boomers! Here are our challenges and opportunities

Why do millennials and younger merely tolerate such a potentially loveable broadcaster as the BBC? Victoria McCollum, who works with this 'lost generation', outlines five reasons why the corporation, despite its admirable efforts, is struggling to engage them

It will make for uncomfortable but necessary reading for the BBC, but worth it. This chapter has insights drawn from my own experience and from group discussions with more than 150 BSc Cinematic Arts students enrolled on my Business of Film and TV module at Ulster University. Prepare yourselves....

1. We are broke and miserable: Lose the licence fee

CHALLENGE: There's a reason why the American-animated sitcom, *Top Cat*, about a hustling homeless chancer, is being used to advertise mortgages for the Halifax. TC, who lives in a back-alley dustbin, and who I engaged with every morning before school as a child, shares our cash-strapped plight. World-weary millennials have ditched television licences for dystopian binges on Netflix. Why? Because, we're saddled with debt, unable to accumulate wealth, and (mostly) stuck in low-benefit, dead-end jobs.

Millennials and younger will never gain the financial security and living standards that our parents (Baby Boomers and Gen X-ers) enjoyed. The year is 2020, a peak earning year according to *Business Insider*, and we find ourselves, once again, marching toward meltdown as we enter an economic cataclysm more severe than the Great Recession. We, the millennials and younger, will be the first generations in modern British history to end up poorer than our parents. We are vulnerable. We are heavily dependent on the gig economy.

Paying a hefty licence fee feels like death by a thousand cuts. Believe me, I know. I once worked as a Complaints Advisor for BBC Audience Services. The truth is, we deeply desire access to the 16 episodes of *Blue Planet* on iPlayer, which is astonishing to watch, but the 28 of +2000 episodes of *Bargain Hunt* available is a deal breaker for us. For millennials and younger, the licence fee is equivalent to on coffee every week for an entire year. That's equivalent to 24 months of Netflix!

OPPORTUNITY: Adopt a Prime video-style subscription model, in place of the licence fee, or lose a generation.

2. We surf whilst we watch: Meet us where we are

CHALLENGE: It feels as if the BBC, despite its efforts, takes a tone-deaf approach to contemporary digital culture. Just as we, the millennials and younger, are required to build a strong online presence in order to engage potential employers, so should the BBC construct a more innovative online persona, integrating popular internet phenomena, to prove worthy of our wallets.

The ways in which the BBC currently engages social media platforms are far from under-30s friendly. For example, my students greatly prefer Vice news' Twitter account (@ViceNews) to the BBC's (@BBCNews), because it feels more like an edgy digital outsider than the slick global empire that it is.

The BBC's official Instagram channel (@BBC) does feature some memes, which is a start, considering millennials and younger use these bottom-up expressions to entertain, inform and educate each other on a daily basis. Memes shape public conversation.

What is most surprising is that the BBC has virtually no presence on the most popular short-form video-sharing apps with cult-followings, like TikTok. Early-career female journalists, like Sophia Smith Galer and Emma Bentley, often share unofficial video content on TikTok about working at the BBC, which regularly goes viral.

However, one can only assume that the efforts of both journalists, who have now accrued more than 12,000 followers, are being ignored by those in the upper echelons of senior management at the BBC, who are, granted, not likely on TikTok.

That said, the broadcaster should be sincerely commended for its latest efforts to engage millennials and younger. Recent BBC news podcast *The Next Episode* genuinely engages with stories that matter to us, as does BBC Three's *Normal People* about love, sex, and class in contemporary Ireland, and new digital video platform *BBC Reel*, which features factual shorts about gender, race, fitness, addiction, psychology and sex. If only this relatable content was not forcibly squeezed through such traditional channels, which often feel stale in style and function to millennials and younger. The dog has mastered the tricks, but its appearance is of consequence too.

OPPORTUNITY: Tell comprehensive stories through multiple reinforcing channels. Invest in original, personal and authentic social content. Bring a strategic and creative approach to social media. We do not expect excessive hashtags, emojis, or phrases like 'it's lit', but we do expect to be retweeted and engaged by questions, polls, sassy replies and irreverent comments. Embrace your place in popular culture. There's a reason why no one wants to 'BBC and chill'. Meet us where we are or lose a generation.

3. We have trust issues: Reinvent quality news

CHALLENGE: Millennials and younger, whilst we adore radio because it feels like a present-tense authentic medium in which events unfold right before our ears, don't trust traditional media and advertising. We are forced to consume it, but its tactics so often comes across as pushy and disingenuous. We look to our network for recommendations – to influencers. We look for social proof in an era saturated with choice. For example, I recently watched Netflix's *Tiger King* due to the recommendation of the masses on my Twitter feed, which tends to feature film and TV academics, critics and friends. 'Fomo' brought me to *Tiger King* – the fear of missing out.

We trust user-generated, personalised content, such as tweets, to a much greater degree than we trust branded content. Video is the differentiator for us – the great empathy machine.

We dig decelerated headlines, which expand, via video, into opportunities for us to deeply connect with people and cultures. Speed-read headlines, such as ';70 killed in suspected chemical attack in Douma', cause us to recoil and disengage.

The BBC's fiercest rivals, such as Vice News and BuzzFeed, immerse us in the action, using innovative journalistic storytelling strategies to build deep empathetic connections with their audiences. Vice News journalists go there, they experience it, they talk about what they see – and they look just like us, as opposed to white, middle-aged men, which fortunately appear to constitute an endangered species on digital media.

Millennials and younger also have powerful bullshit detectors. We know when we're being sold a piece of commoditised information, which is a slave to editorial guidelines, over a sincere opinion or perspective. We want to know what people think. We dig multi-perspectivity. Storytelling is important to us. We want to hear original stories – sociologically-relevant conversation-starters – not so dictated to by broadcast rules or advertisers.

Millennials and younger want to consume editorial that involves a deep integration of tech, from genuinely pro-digital culture news outlets that do not feel particularly nostalgic about the good old (legacy news) days.

OPPORTUNITY: The BBC has been active in the digital field for 26 years now; it has learned about how this space functions, and is attuned to the pace of the industry and how innovation is best approached. Engage, via immersive journalism, with the issues that traditional outlets are known not to engage with, such as antifascist youth movements, student protests, cutting-edge new art forms, cannabis, new-age health, the world's oppressed, and LGBT culture. Anchor and steer your news with young and relatable on-air correspondents who appear to take on the establishment or lose a generation.

4. We cultivate a culture of inclusion: Concentrate on reach not ratings

CHALLENGE: Millennials and younger are more connected to global citizenship and human rights than nationalism. We are morally minded and ethically informed global citizens that enjoy genre-defining and boundary-pushing content.

For us, the BBC so often seems to care more about ratings than it does reach. Millennials and younger know only too well that minority ethnic groups, LBGT people and those with disabilities make up a shameful percentage of the BBC's creative workforce and we assume this discrepancy bleeds into programming.

When in search of British content, my students often turn to Channel 4 for an authentic portrayal of their lives, claiming that the BBC fails to connect with their spine – "it feels white, middle class, mostly concerned with the South East."

On the other hand, we know that the BBC's competitors target programming at specific demographics using viewership data. Believe me, I was working at HBO in NYC when it launched its on-demand streaming service HBO Go, which was the result of micro-profiling, micro-targeting and micro-aggregation on a global scale – something in which Netflix and Amazon Prime also have unique expertise.

Where is the BBC's insatiable appetite for data-gathering, which would help the broadcaster to ring-fence funds for diverse programming? Recently, and in reference to audience data and algorithms, BBC Director of Content Charlotte Moore stated, "I don't believe any amount of data can tell you what to commission next."

Why on earth not? Is it not one of the BBC's core public purposes to reflect and serve the UK's diverse communities? Perhaps, data-led decision making would allow the BBC to recognise that its audience is increasingly diverse. After all, why would a viewer want to watch programmes that consistently fail to resonate with any of their personal experiences?

OPPORTUNITY: The BBC should focus on the reach of specific programmes over audience size. True inclusion does not start and end, for example, with token casting. 'Progressive' re-imaginings of shows like *Doctor Who*, for instance, are emblematic of the problem: attempting to rewrite the past, instead of looking to the future.

Diversity is not a varnish you can apply to old familiar stories. Millennials and younger crave an expanded universe. Take responsibility for ensuring improved balance through in-house measuring of progress on equality and internal reflection on that progress. Integrate cultural diversity, inclusion and equity into all aspects of your operations or lose a generation.

5. Quality TV is important to us: Make more TV that no longer resembles TV

CHALLENGE: Millennials and younger look for experiences over possessions. We are lured in by networks with strong legitimisation strategies, such as 'It's not TV, it's HBO', which ultimately promise a high-quality viewing experience.

For us, quality TV is best defined by what it is not 'regular television'. In fact, the less television resembles television – the more we like it. Netflix is well aware of this. There is a reason why the term 'Original' is front and centre of its own promotional discourses. We want novelty, originality, prestige – new storytelling practices unimaginable in the past.

Give us television that appeals to us technologically and aesthetically and we will binge, and feast on it. Millennials and younger rate Toms over Nike because we believe that the brand's purpose is to create world value, not just shareholder value.

In other words, its purpose aligns with what's important to us. The BBC has a well-established reputation for culturally valuable programming. Millennials and younger see this expressed most explicitly in the content of BBC Four. Why? Because it feels as if the depth and substance of content on the channel is made to appeal to a much narrower audience with specific tastes, than, say, the content of BBC Two, which is much too broad to interest us.

Millennials and younger are used to being classified and identified as an audience through the use of narrow frameworks. Sharpened storytelling is the new black. We adore programming that creatively engages with genre material, leans toward the controversial and realistic, experiments with narrative complexity and breaks the established rules of television.

Give us something to think about. Give us sharp social and cultural criticism. I have had more water-cooler conversations with my students about *Fleabag* (BBC Three), *Gentleman Jack* (BBC One), *Killing Eve* (BBC One) and *Twin* (BBC Four) in the last year than I have had about any other programmes.

OPPORTUNITY: Invest in a narrow range of expensive, high-end distinctively British stories that millennials and younger can anticipate before broadcast and savour afterward. Instead of seeking to educate, inform and entertain us, enlighten, challenge and involve us – and gain a generation. We deeply want to belong to a broadcaster that deeply wants us to belong.

About the writer

Dr Victoria McCollum is an award-wining lecturer in Cinematic Arts at Ulster University, Northern Ireland, and has previously held positions at BBC, ITV, MTV and HBO. She has published several cutting-edge books on film, media and television, such as *HBO's Original Voices: Race, Gender, Sexuality and Power* (2018); *Make America Hate Again: Trump-Era Horror and the Politics of Fear* (2019); and *#Resist: Protest and Resistance Media in Trump-Era USA* (2020). Victoria believes in engaging students as partners and is dedicated to creating transformative learning opportunities for her students encouraging them to develop their own identities as filmmakers, producers and content creators. You can find her on Twitter: @Vic_McC.

Vox Populi

Caitlin Caldwell, 16, student, County Antrim

I mainly watch BBC content through the BBC iPlayer app. I find this particularly useful as it allows me to watch programmes I might have missed throughout the week, without the inconvenience of advertisements.

However, I do occasionally enjoy watching the news on BBC One.

My friends and I enjoy watching a wide range of programmes on the BBC, although we believe that there may be a gap within the service for young people our age (16-18 year olds). On a whole, there are some interesting series available, but we would appreciate if the BBC catered to our age range with a more light-hearted, modern genre.

Personally, I would miss the wide range of gripping crime dramas aired as well as the convenience of the catch-up service.

Although I'm not of licence-paying age, I believe that the BBC is good value for money as the catch-up service is available at no extra cost. The BBC could be better value for money if it introduced a movie-streaming service.

I believe the BBC could employ more current, up-to-date celebrities, recognised by young people, to be involved in their advertising campaigns, as well as the addition of some new programmes/ podcasts aimed at teenagers.

The worst thing about the BBC to me personally, is the lack of comedic, light-hearted content as the serious dramas don't suit everyone. I believe that the BBC may be more appealing to young people if it aired some popular movies aimed at teenagers.

Chapter 3

There's still a role in our national life

While the BBC faces multiple threats to its existence, it remains an important and vital part of our cultural ecosystem. While it must be smarter about how it uses its resources, it is well advised to continue to serve as wide a demographic as possible, writes Ed Vaizey

After the 2015 election, John Whittingdale was appointed as Culture Secretary. The BBC Charter was up for renewal, and John's appointment was seen as a clear signal to the Tory right that the Cameron government was prepared to be tough on the BBC. I remained in post, as John's junior minister and 'soft cop'.

In fact it was much more nuanced than that. John had been a distinguished chairman of the Commons select committee covering the Department for Culture, Media and Sport (DCMS), and knows as much as anyone about media. He is not knee-jerk anti the BBC.

I was far more sceptical about the BBC than people perceived. I had even managed a *Sunday Times* front page, when I was Opposition spokesman, for musing unguardedly about the desirability of privatising Radio 1. I was not simply a cheerleader for the corporation.

My own thoughts on Radio 1 summed up the fundamental paradox at the heart of the BBC's mission.

On the one hand, it receives a massive public subsidy, which protects it from market forces. So one would expect it to use that funding to pay for the content and services that would not otherwise be commercial. Hence the scepticism over Radio 1. On the other hand, everyone pays the licence fee, so quite reasonably the BBC believes it should provide something for everyone – from *Strictly* to *Gardener's World.*

There, too, lies another problem for the BBC. Because everyone pays, everyone has an opinion, and it quickly descends into what programmes one likes, and what programmes one hates. Policy is driven by anecdote.

As I write, I think of the Vaizey family viewing habits. I am binge-watching Netflix, but also listening to Radio 4 and watching BBC drama. My children are using TikTok and You Tube, but also occasionally sitting down en famille to watch Auntie. To make things harder, the BBC's news coverage ensures that MPs and policy makers remain in a permanent funk, convinced that the BBC is biased against their side, because it doesn't report the news exactly as they want it.

The process of Charter review

In 2015, Charter review looked simple enough. I joked that we could get it through in a week, and after a convoluted process that is in effect what we did, albeit with one or two disastrous last-minute hits.

Reform of regulation was long overdue, and we abolished the BBC Trust and replaced it with Ofcom, giving much more independent oversight. The BBC had long resisted this but, as I always knew it would be, the transition was smooth and so far seems to have been successful. We wanted to check the licence fee was still the right way to fund the BBC, and, as I suspected, we concluded that it was the least worst option, and still had some life in it. It remains largely accepted by the public and ensures the BBC's independence.

The BBC had some wins. We successfully saw off attempts to decriminalise non-payment of the licence fee. It successfully resisted our call to sell its stake in UKTV (it now wholly owns it); it was given freedom to build up BBC Studios as a commercial operation; and we stopped asking it to contribute to the funding of broadband roll-out. Finally, the licence fee was also increased.

But there were some damaging changes as well. We now require the BBC to put every programme out to tender, which is time consuming for the BBC and prevents it building up a store of IP. We use some licence-fee money to fund programmes made by other broadcasters, which confuses the point of the licence fee. It is neither fish nor fowl – too small to make a difference to other broadcasters, but a breach of the principle that the licence fee should fund the BBC.

By far the most damaging, of course, was the decision to make the BBC responsible for the free licence fee for the over-75s, which will have a massive and severe impact on the corporation. It is completely without principle. The over-75s licence fee was a decision taken by government, and should continue to be funded by government. Any changes to its scope should also be decided by the government, not out-sourced to the BBC.

Current challenges

Nevertheless, the BBC has lived to fight another day. But it now faces a war on many fronts.

The over-75s issue has not been resolved, and will have an ever increasing and massive impact on its finances. The rise of Netflix and other streaming services threatens the BBC in two ways. Not only are they competing for viewers, but their budgets for making programmes dwarf the BBC's and pushes up the cost of production. And the plethora of new media channels, from TikTok to YouTube, means that the BBC risks losing more and more viewers, particularly the young.

In its recent annual report, the BBC has suggested that it will return BBC Three, its dedicated youth channel, to linear broadcasting. When it was moved on-line, I supported the change, seeing it as a bold move to get ahead of changes in viewing habits. But many people in TV-land opposed it – one even offered to buy it. They recognised that the programmes they make for the channel often succeed because of serendipity – people coming across them by chance. They have welcomed the change in heart.

I am not a broadcaster, and I have never run a television company. Politicians (and ex-politicians, in my case) aren't qualified to make strategic decisions about what the BBC should do to maintain viewers, or to win over particular demographics. But it seems to me there are a couple of principles which politicians can adhere to when considering how and whether to support the BBC.

First, the multi-media environment in which we live is dominated by US culture. There is something to be said for a degree of cultural autonomy (one to which the French in particular are wedded to). Without the BBC, and the subsidy it receives, we would see much less UK homegrown cultural content. I think it is essential that we maintain it, and the BBC is best placed to do that.

Related to this, the BBC remains a developer of training for talent; a catalyst for constant innovation (not least the wild success of the iPlayer); and an important source of commissions for UK production companies. All of these will be undermined by a diminished BBC.

Second, the BBC does stuff for young people which commercial broadcasters find difficult. In particular, its children's programming is essential viewing and a lifeline for parents. I think it's particularly important for young children to grow up with culturally-relevant programming, not an endless diet of American cartoons.

A way forward

While the BBC cannot stop the young migrating to other channels and platforms, it can do much more to engage a young audience.

My kids are wedded to a string of influencers and YouTubers who appear to have no relationship with the BBC at all. I am unclear if the BBC is getting out of its comfort zone of engaging with the big and established indies to engage with them. Certainly, it should be looking at commissioning content from them.

This new landscape also gives the BBC the chance to move away from being a closed platform.

If original BBC content is available on TikTok or YouTube, this is as far as I am concerned still the BBC. This crystallises the need for the BBC to think hard about whether it is a platform or a content provider, or a judicious mix of the two. At the moment the BBC is skewed too far to being a closed platform.

In addition, the BBC must decide what its core services are. In the debate, not enough attention is paid to BBC local radio which carries out a vital service – there should be more, not less, investment here. As for national radio, it seems to me that Radios 3, 4, 5 and 6 are important, as is Asian radio. But while I love Radios 1 and 2 I still can't see what they are doing that commercial radio couldn't. Much of what they provide could be realised through a partnership with commercial radio, where commercial radio carried some of the very good public service content that does indeed appear on these stations.

Oh, and all the BBC's national stations should be digital-only.

In 2022, the BBC celebrates its centenary. It is remarkable that it is still here, and that it remains the dominant broadcaster and a force for good in our national life. But like all successful businesses, it must change and adapt to secure its survival.

About the writer

Ed Vaizey was Minister for Culture from 2010-16. He was responsible for overseeing the review of the BBC Charter in 2015. Ed left parliament in 2019 and now advises a range of clients in media and technology policy. @edvaizey vaizeye@gmail.com

Sound bite #2

Baroness Morgan of Cotes (Nicky Morgan), Secretary of State for Digital, Culture, Media and Sport, 2019-2020

In short, the BBC needs to appeal to all ages and to build up a following amongst younger viewers to ensure they become the older, more committed viewers of tomorrow.

It is hard to prescribe what the remedy is but I expect the BBC must take regular soundings from the age group, but also understand that they seem to be a generation which prefers to dip in and out of a service. which is why streaming works for them rather than the commitment of an annual licence fee.

Chapter 4

Dangerously close to the brink? Or not?

Far from being a lost generation, the evidence is that a younger audience will come to the BBC when they are offered must-see content on a platform to which they can relate, says Peter Weil

An internal BBC document warns that the broadcaster is 'dangerously close to the brink' over its failure to attract young viewers. Ofcom predicts that "the BBC may not be sustainable in its current form if it fails to regain younger audiences who are increasingly tuning out of its services". So what's going on?

Periodically, certain BBC executives and the opinion formers with whom they dine join forces to convince themselves that a part of the output faces an existential crisis.

Watchdog, for example, is one of the mainstays of BBC One but 30 years ago, when I was offered the post of Head of Topical Features, it was on the understanding that I axed the series. True, it needed a rethink and a fresh coat of paint, but any weaknesses were far outweighed by its strengths. So, once I was safely ensconced in my new role, I conveniently forgot all about the instruction and instead persuaded the talented Sarah Caplin to take on the role of editor. The rest is history.

Yes, the BBC needs to improve its efforts to connect with a younger audience, but the facts suggest that – just like *Watchdog* – Armageddon is some distance away.

When the BBC comes up with a hit, the evidence suggests that the youth audience will find it. Radio 1 for example reaches 10m listeners. *Normal People* has been a breakout hit. *Peaky Blinders* is regularly watched by more than 40 per cent of 16-34-year-olds while *Noughts and Crosses, Dracula,* and *My Mate's A Bad Date* all attracted healthy audiences.

In 2019 the BBC One peak-time share for the 16-34 years demographic rose by more than four per cent to reach a healthy 17 per cent.

While it's not surprising that TV audiences rose during lockdown, what is newsworthy is that between mid-March and mid-April this year, BBC One's share of the youth audience increased considerably. The biggest growth was for the 10pm news bulletin. The challenge now is how to maintain that spike.

News for a youth audience

Twenty-five years ago, Channel Four Schools invited indies to pitch for a news programme to be targeted at a younger audience. The budget was modest, and most companies saw the commission as a licence to lose money.

At the time I was the Head of Development at Barraclough Carey and persuaded ITN's team at Channel 4 News to join us in the bid. Simultaneously we signed two top children's producers – Madeleine Wiltshire and Louise Lynch – to come on board.

Each edition would consist of a film presented by one of our viewers and directed by either Louise or Maddie, a C4 News report from one of their correspondents specifically targeted at a younger audience and an interview with a news maker, conducted by two of our viewers. Jon Snow agreed to front the programme and was happy to share the interviewer's role with the young people. It was their interview but if the interviewee refused to answer the questions or worse still, attempted to patronise our junior reporters, Jon would step in with a killer supplementary.

The format worked well but we believed our programme deserved a larger audience than Schools could provide on its own. With the support of C4 Schools, we also pitched the series to C4's children's commissioning editor. We offered a Saturday update targeted at a wider audience but at no extra cost. The series aired three times a week, attracted a respectable audience and ran for almost a decade.

Things may well have changed now but, at the time, it would have been impossible to have pitched such a series to the BBC. A joint production between BBC news, involving its key anchor, the children's department, the schools' department and an independent production company would simply have been unthinkable. The internal politics alone would have been horrendous. But by staying below the radar and working with Channel 4, we were able to deliver.

I'm not suggesting resurrecting *First Edition* on the BBC. However, the BBC currently has two daily news services that are specifically targeted at young people – Radio 1's *Newsbeat* and CBBC's *Newsround*. While *Newsbeat* goes from strength to strength and produces its own documentaries for the iPlayer, *Newsround*'s slots have been significantly reduced. Maybe after almost four decades, *Newsround* has had its day. Why not amalgamate its resources with those of *Newsbeat*?

Newsbeat, which is already producing documentaries for the i-player, could become the BBC's flagship news programme for the younger audience and build up the brand across all its platforms, supported by significant cross-promotion. The success of *First Edition* demonstrates the importance of ignoring traditional fiefdoms.

Lessons from Northern Ireland

One of the strongest arguments for regional broadcasting is an ability to serve a diverse youth audience.

Back in 1984 I was blissfully unaware that Northern Ireland even had a youth programmes unit. I was a producer on *Newsnight* when, out of the blue, Cecil Taylor, the Belfast-based Head of Programmes, invited me to consider applying for the job as head of department. I spluttered something to the effect that I knew nothing about rock music, didn't inhale and was totally unsuitable for the job. "Young man," responded Taylor, somewhat indignantly, "if I wanted someone knowledgeable about the rock scene, I would not be approaching you."

Maybe because of my reservations I was appointed to the job and discovered quickly that no one resents the concept of youth programmes as much as young people themselves. They are not a homogeneous group. Many regard the concept as patronising, especially if faced with an ageing producer dressed in equally ageing jeans who is desperately trying to pretend that he is one of them.

We decided to offer a diverse range of different programmes to cater for as many varied interests as possible. We sought a team of young people who were passionate about the prospect and already showed that initial vital spark of talent. My role was to identify the talent who by virtue of being part of the community identified with the target audience and understood their tastes.

Our team members went on to make their mark in the industry – be it running two of Northern Ireland's most successful indies; becoming president of Comedy Central in New York; vice president of BBC America; a presenter on Radio 4's *Sunday* or *Blue Peter*; a reporter on *Animal Hospital*; a producer on *Panorama;* or the main anchor on *ITV Weekend News.*

Some years later I worked with six groups of young people in Northern Ireland to produce a range of short films told from the point of view of local groups, such as the gay community, travellers and the homeless. The films were shown in a local cinema but once again we wanted to see if we could reach a larger audience.

I approached the ITV region in the shape of UTV's then Director of Programmes (the co-editor of this book) to see if he was interested. He politely explained that unlike the BBC, UTV was a commercial channel. I made him an offer: "We'll give you the films for free if in return you give us a day of studio and editing time to assemble the programme for free. And if you opt out of the network and air the programme in the 10.40 slot, I guarantee you will beat the network slot average." I crossed my fingers.

The executive was so intrigued by the chutzpah that he agreed. Much to everyone's amazement, my promise came good and I was able to uncross my fingers.

Developing a channel of the year

Both initiatives worked because our young people were at the heart of the operation. It was their passion and talent which drove the programmes. My role was to support them but not to impose my views on how to connect with the audience.

At the 2017 Bafta Children's Awards ceremony, on-line education channel TrueTube was the surprise victor. It not only won Children's Channel of the Year, the first time the category went to an on-line only channel, but also picked up three further Baftas for its films. How did it do it and what are the lessons for the BBC?

There was a desperate need for reliable content for religious education (RE) classes. An Ofsted report highlighted concerns that RE teaching was suffering from a lack of teachers with specialist qualifications.

Nick Stuart, my predecessor as CEO at CTVC, a company which specialises in social issues, current affairs, religion and ethics, spotted an opportunity. TrueTube was launched with a brief to provide RE classes and their teachers with much-needed support.

In a different climate and at a different time it would have been the BBC which would have attempted to address the challenge, but a schools' series which focused on religion seemed distinctly unappetising. The path was open for CTVC. But how did it manage to win Channel of the Year?

When I inherited CTVC, my priority was to recruit the most amazing array of talent; people who were hungry, passionate, dedicated and had something of an X factor about them. They included Adam Tyler who worked for four years with us creating short dramas and documentaries, and who during that time won five Baftas; Bob Ayres, who joined as an education producer and who previously had successfully run three RE departments at different schools and bought unique authority, knowledge and experience to the project; and Stuart Porter who held the whole enterprise together as well as raising the necessary funding from various EU sources.

My concluding thought is that every challenge also offers a solution. Given that most teenagers appear to prefer to watch YouTube or TikTok rather than BBC Three, we should take advantage of the fact that BBC Studios is encouraged to pitch outside the BBC.

The question is whether the BBC is primarily trying to drive viewers to its content or its platforms. If to the former, BBC Studios' priority should be to pitch to those platforms which the younger audience are watching. Miraculously the figures for consumption of BBC content by a young audience will then go up and the prophets of doom will, in turn, have had their day.

About the writer

Peter Weil started work on children's programmes almost six decades ago when he first played a dog on the BBC Home Service's *Children's Hour* and progressed to the role of Minoru a Japanese boy who was kidnapped.

He then spent more than 40 years in broadcasting. His experience includes Head of Youth Programmes for BBC Northern Ireland; executive producer for *Wogan*; senior vice president, Discovery Networks International; and CEO, CTVC which is part of the Rank Foundation.

He is currently the CEO of the Northern Ireland based Politics in Action, which offers shared education classes in politics to secondary schools and a governor of Stranmillis University College.

Vox Populi

Christopher Hudson, 13, student, County Durham

The BBC feels old and outdated. It needs to feel more like the streaming services Netflix and Amazon Prime.

It's great there are box sets on the iPlayer but there needs to be more. I want to watch content anytime, not wait for the next episodes to have been on television.

In the morning I listen to BBC radio – Radio 2 as my parents are listening then. After that I use the smart TV and iPlayer for other content at other times – I don't watch much live tv.

Debates on the BBC are very good, and one of the real positives is there are no advertisements.

Chapter 5

It's all doable – but will the BBC do it?

The BBC has a fight on its hands to stem audience losses to competitors. It needs to sharpen both its content offering and its technology so that there is something for every element of Britain's diverse population. An historical lack of innovation, an unfocused product range and an inflated cost base have stopped it doing this to date. Alison Dolan hopes it can change

Many of the audience challenges faced by the BBC are far from unique to it. How to grow the overall audience, how to address the increased fragmentation of content supply, how to set the organisation up to ride the wave of change – these are all issues faced by every media brand in the world.

Within that, the particular challenge of how to engage young people while retaining their parents (and grandparents) is also an enormous challenge for everyone. And it is particularly acute with the younger generation who have such a wide choice of content providers and a multitude of devices on which to discover content outside the UK's traditional TV and radio landscapes.

As the battleground increasingly moves to the phone, media brands are also competing with games, music, social feeds, e-sports – as well as video aggregators like YouTube. The old delineations between viewing times and reading times are blurred or removed entirely, and melting into a battle for attention on mobile. Amidst all this competition, giving young people a reason to spend time with your brand is something that needs thought and focus.

The BBC's unique funding model makes finding some actionable answers crucial to its ongoing viability. A disengaged generation of young people may not evolve into a willing licence-fee paying generation, and the public purpose of the BBC is also called into question if large subgroups of the population never interact with its content. A problem which has traditionally self-corrected as young people grow up is increasingly unlikely to continue to do so going forward, so it is certainly an issue that should concern both the BBC and Ofcom.

I wonder though if the problem really is one of youth engagement, or a set of unrealistic expectations for the extent of youth engagement with any one brand. The popularity of shows like *Fleabag*, *Killing Eve*, *Strictly Come Dancing*, *Bodyguard*, the engagement with live sport and the BBC's music channels are all clear evidence that the right content, surfaced in the right way, will get young people watching BBC content. There is no evidence of prejudice against the BBC in the minds of young people – they are happy to watch when there is something they want to watch.

But, with the explosion of broadcasters, streamers, video aggregators and content budgets, it is no longer realistic for any one broadcaster to expect to be all things to all people, or to expect an individual show to engage every section of the viewing population.

There is no winner takes all end-state where one broadcaster or channel is every viewer's default. Success going forward will be show-by-show, event-by-event, the quality bar will rise ever higher, and loyalty will be to shows rather than to broadcasters or to channels.

It is a shift that is great for consumer choice, but it has consequences in viewing behaviour. The linear schedule becomes far less important – particularly for young people – as on-demand and time-shifted viewing take over; the need to make relevant content easy to find becomes far more important and, if engaging a particular subgroup of the population is an objective, then making content that skews to their interests and then ensuring they can find it easily becomes the challenge, rather than maintaining a pre-set number of linear channels, which need to be padded with less expensive, but less engaging content.

There is one certainty – the licence fee will not be increasing! In that context, a strong content strategy for both the schedule and the iPlayer to create a diverse programming output, with focus on ensuring there is always something for every interest, may go a long way to addressing the problem.

The pillars of the strategy I think are needed at this point are the following:

- technical innovation in products and smart tech partnerships;
- a much sharper content strategy; reflecting the interests of a segmented audience;
- a social media strategy which amplifies the content investment and engages young people on other platforms;
- a ruthless cost-reduction programme to maximise content budgets. The BBC is seen as fat and inefficient. Waste can be cut in news gathering and production, sports coverage, and management layers through removal of duplication and wasted investment.

In the current fragmented broadcast landscape, how broadcasters help their viewers to discover content and biggest differentiators in quality of the user experience. This will only increase as we go forward.

Netflix, Sky and Spotify, in particular, have brilliantly created slick user interfaces and algorithms to help their viewers and listeners to navigate content and to personalise the content recommendations. They make content easy to find, and easy to view or listen to on the move, and on multiple devices, which has encouraged their viewers to spend more time with their content.

For the BBC, this is the sort of user experience that their viewers and listeners – especially younger viewers – are being offered by their competitors and are being trained to expect, but they are not getting it from the BBC. The iPlayer, innovative when it was first introduced, is now outdated and clunky. Content is hard to find, and the mix of linear and iPlayer-only content is unclear. It needs investment and overhaul to make it a destination in the way that Netflix or the Sky homepages are.

Content strategy

BBC Sounds has been a promising start in consolidating the BBC's audio output and keeping it from TuneIn and Spotify, but it needs to evolve its personalisation capabilities and increase functionality. It has already built a strong stable of investigative, documentary and comedy podcasts, should continue to do so, and a sharp user experience will complement the content.

Likewise, BritBox is an example of the sort of commercial partnership innovation that the BBC needs to do more of. Deeper tech partnerships may also help to accelerate its capabilities or reduce the cost of building its own.

Go big on UK drama; develop a proper strategy for live sport, revamp what is currently dull but trustworthy news, kill the channel-fillers.

As we head towards a world of loyalty to shows rather than to channels or to broadcasters, content budgets need to prioritise shows that count – that engage new and existing viewers across the full UK population – and make every show count. Competition is ferocious and the US streamers have both deep pockets and other products with which to cross-subsidise and cross-promote their TV investments.

Here in the UK, Sky has recently announced a new set of studios at Elstree, £3bn of (new) production investment in the UK with 80 new drama originals in the coming year; Netflix content spending in 2020 will top $17bn; Disney+ is predicted to do the same; Apple and Amazon will each spend $6bn on original shows.

So the BBC needs to play to its strengths, as well to its obligations as a British public service provider (PSB).

Drama should remain a priority, the BBC does it really well and it engages different generations and ethnicities. Fundamental to the BBC's purpose is creating British content, reflecting British culture and British people and this is so important when enormous content budgets sit in the US.

It is also content that exports well globally. BBC Studios and creative partnerships such as its partnership with Amazon for *Fleabag* need to be used to their fullest extent.

Outside drama, the BBC's brilliance at natural world and hard-hitting documentaries gives it a natural advantage over other broadcasters – who also do less of this type of content – and they should remain priorities, as should its brilliant range of comedy. These are all programming genres that help to justify the licence fee.

On the other side of that coin, however, reality shows, makeovers, game-shows and soaps lower the quality bar of BBC1 and BBC2. They are too similar to the output of the other UK PSBs and do little to bring in new and different sectors of the population. Padding channels with schedule-fillers needs to stop, the number of channels reduced and each remaining channel made more compelling than it currently is.

Segment the audience and ensure that there is enough content for each group.

Content performance needs to be measured; the purpose of each show and its contribution – not just to growing the overall audience – but to building a diverse audience across the full spectrum of ages, genders, regions and ethnicities, needs to be established, understood and assessed. Shows that don't perform need to be axed.

There is too much competition, too large a supply of great content and too great a need to put every available penny into content that engages people. Yes, the linear schedule needs to be filled (ideally with fewer than four channels), but filled with the acknowledgement that it is irrelevant to many elements of the audience – therefore being done as cost-efficiently as possible in order to create as many great flagship shows as possible and to maximise the value of content budgets.

Coverage of live sport needs a major rethink – both the extent of events covered and the quality of the coverage. This is particularly so when events beyond the Group A listed events are involved. Spending licence-fee money and competing with the likes of Sky and BT Sport for live rights is divisive – on the one hand they bring families and different generations together, but on the other (and depending on the event), many licence fee payers have little interest and resent the money required both to acquire the rights and then to cover them, not only on television, but on radio also.

Added to this, the BBC's coverage of live sport is not always particularly good. Events like the Masters, which are shared with Sky, make it easy to compare slick, technical and innovative coverage and commentary with the BBC's staid alternative.

Everyone will have a view on which individual live events the BBC should cover, but the important point is that the corporation itself needs to decide and be clear about which events are important to the British public, ensuring sufficient diversity of events, and then reinvigorate its coverage. Do less and do it better.

There is also so much more that the BBC could do to make its news coverage more engaging and pushing home its real advantage in this area. As a brand, it is more trusted than any other news provider in the UK. In times such as these, or during any other major event, more people turn to the BBC than to any other news brand. This makes life difficult for other news media – particularly when it comes to breaking news coverage – but it's also an advantage that the BBC doesn't do enough to capitalise on.

In more normal times, fewer and fewer people are engaging with television news in the UK at all – particularly outside London. It has evolved very little in format and presentation over the last 40 years, despite the advances in other programming, and it has none of the colour and flair we see in our newspapers.

Many viewers, particularly outside large metropolitan areas, do not see their lives reflected in the topics selected for coverage and the way in which they are addressed. Left-wing bias; the worthiness and political correctness that saw scandals like Rotherham underexposed; the Brexit immigration issues tiptoed-around and misrepresented as racism; the preachiness of London-based Remainer presenters – were all particularly exposed during both the Brexit debate and the 2019 election and they have undermined the BBC's impartiality; large elements of the population have switched off and are happy to get their news from Facebook and echo chambers like Twitter.

Viewers may have temporarily switched back, but once the corona crisis is over, they won't stay. It's not just a BBC problem – the same is true of Sky News and ITN – but real British people's lives and the issues that matter to them need to be covered without fear and by people that a broader proportion of the British population see as relevant and reflective of themselves. The BBC can, and must, lead this change.

Social media strategy and costs

A coherent social media strategy is also required – again where there is a clear purpose and target audience for each account. Instagram alone currently has 11 different BBC accounts, some for individual channels, some for individual shows, one even for the iPlayer. It is difficult to see what they are doing and who they are designed to appeal to, but the purpose should be to complement and amplify the content output in a way that is appropriate for the particular platform.

Radical action is needed! The waste, duplication, lack of resource-sharing at the BBC are legendary at other broadcasters. Multiple teams from different stations and channels sent to cover the same event; larger teams than any other broadcaster; very few of the cost-cutting measures seen in newsrooms and broadcast production teams elsewhere are evident yet at the BBC. It does not think and behave like a commercial organisation.

But with so much competition, it is absolutely imperative that the money available for quality programming is maximised, not wasted through inefficiency. Managers with expertise from commercial broadcasters should be brought in or consulted about making the BBC and its operations far leaner. Even licence-fee supporters balk at the idea that the cost base is higher than it needs to be and that waste can be removed without touching the quality of the programming. This is an absolute priority.

In summary

The good news is that everything is actionable, with the right mindset. The BBC is far from being a toxic brand, which is off-putting to young people and needs to be rescued. A world where public engagement with its content is broad, licence-fee renewal is more secure because more people are satisfied with the service they receive; and the PSB remit and the division between PSBs and their commercial rivals is less of an issue than it is currently is achievable.

The not so good news is that it is a major challenge. Everything set out here requires the BBC to change in some really fundamental ways, to accept that there are no sacred cows, that historical ways of working need to change because the world around them has changed, and it hasn't done enough to keep pace with that change.

But, there are already some promising innovations, some evidence that it is now pointed in the right direction. Its strong apprenticeship and trainee programs already help to make the BBC accessible to young people.

Content evolution to reflect more of the lives and experiences of young people in Britain today and technological experiences that match those they receive elsewhere are now the next steps in bringing the BBC closer to its young public.

About the writer

Alison Dolan was the chief strategy officer for News UK from 2016 to May 2020. Her primary responsibilities involved working to secure the integration of the Wireless Group, acquired by News UK in 2016; the development of subscription strategies for *The Times/Sunday Times*; the management of News UK's relationship with the large tech platforms and the organisational design of the company.

Prior to News UK, Alison spent 15 years at Sky, where she held a variety of roles including group treasurer, director of finance for technology and deputy managing director for Sky Business, from 2012-2016. She is an Irish national, and lives in south west London with her two daughters.

Sound bite #3

Daisy Cooper, MP for St Albans. Liberal Democrat spokesperson on digital, culture, media and sport

There is clear evidence of changing media habits amongst the under 30s, who are less likely to watch linear TV or listen to radio and more likely to watch streaming services such as Netflix and Amazon Prime and listen to podcasts.

For any universal method of payment to remain viable – whether it be the licence fee, as at present, or some other household-based tax – it's important for BBC services to reach the whole population.

While it's too early to tell whether younger generations will carry their current media consumption habits through to later life, there is certainly a risk. If the BBC were to do nothing to cater for these audiences, there is a strong possibility that they would be more reluctant as they become licence payers and householders themselves to pay for an organisation that that they believe has no relevance to them.

Having said that, it's very important that the BBC does not become fixated on younger audiences at the expense of the vast majority of licence payers.

Ofcom data show that more than 90m per cent of the population access some BBC services at least once a week, and is vital that – in order to sustain its vital contribution at the heart of British culture and democracy – it continues to engage every demographic.

It is a delicate balancing act which the BBC has so far negotiated successfully, and the enormous popularity of both its news and education services during the Covid crisis has demonstrated its enduring role, and that of all public service broadcasters, in the nation's life.

There is no single 'magic bullet' initiative that will attract the under 30s, but two complementary approaches should help to cement the BBC in their lives.

The first is to maintain its investment in popular music through Radio1, with a particular emphasis on new artists and bands which tend to be ignored by commercial radio playlists. The BBC has an excellent track record in launching new musical talent through schemes like BBC Introducing, which helps to invigorate the country's music culture as well as attracting young audiences. Obviously, this would need to include podcasts and other platforms like voice recognition (such as Alexa).

The second, it needs to maintain – and if possible increase – its investment in original drama that will attract this generation. Shows like Normal People and Fleabag have generated huge admiration for their originality and quality, and it was a great shame that the BBC felt it necessary to remove BBC Three from its linear schedule.

This strategy is now being rethought as part of the effort to engage young audiences, and hopefully we'll see it back on the linear schedule alongside BBCs 1, 2 and 4. It's also worth noting that those shows, despite being targeted at young people, have stimulated interest from a much broader demographic – which, indeed, is very much part of the BBC's attraction as an institution capable of surprising all age groups.

It is worth adding that, of course, the BBC must not lose sight of its crucial news and information role: its trust and appreciation ratings have remained high across the board, and the evidence suggests that young people have been just as likely as older age groups to access BBC services for reliable information during the Covid lockdown.

In that sense the BBC, as the pre-eminent public service broadcaster, remains as relevant to the under 30s as all other audiences.

Chapter 6

A Tardis and a flower

A story of fragmentation, disintermediation, and the quest for relevancy. Kerensa Jennings draws on her personal experiences working at the BBC for 15 years to shine a light on risk-taking, vision, technology and storytelling

"Disintermediation," the young strategist said, proud, I think, to have got all the syllables out in one go. "Disintermediation is the future, and the world in 2016 is going to be a completely different place."

That was in 2012. BBC White City building. A salmon pink room. Paint peeling and a tired poster limping off a pin board. A few of us clustered in a too-hot room and everyone wearing earnest expressions. No, not a scene out of comedy show *W1A*. Though it might as well have been.

We'd gathered to watch a whizzy Keynote presentation. It sticks in my memory because I'd never seen Keynote before and the strategist had gone to town on the transitions. It was also the first time I had heard the term "disintermediation".

The deck introduced us to The Future, a foreign place where content would glide around the World Wide Web and everyone from Apple to Amazon would be competing for eyeballs. Distribution channels would seamlessly meld into one another so that no matter your device or location, you could carry on watching, carry on listening, carry on consuming.

The BBC would know everything about each and every person using its products and services, and use AI to make recommendations about what you might like to watch or download based on what you'd done before.

Competitors – traditional rivals like Sky, ITV, Channels 4 and 5 – would be joined by natively digital Goliaths like Netflix, Google, YouTube. Big data would underpin both business and content decisions.

Third party platforms would risk pushing the BBC into a new role. Less content creator and more content provider. We could end up being a library. The iPlayer would be accessed via other people's platforms. People would stop coming to us directly.

And if that happened, how would we justify the licence fee? Our Royal Charter?

Our existence?

Jackdaws

A few years earlier I was in another meeting. With the very brilliant Creative Director of the BBC. In those days, we called the TV part of the BBC 'Vision'. He asked me to create something that would inspire BBC creatives to take risks, and discover the power of digital storytelling, convergence and transmedia content propositions. "I want jackdaws", he said to me.

What he meant was bolder, more innovative approaches to programme making. Taking the best bits from all over the place and making something different. Striving for relevancy. He said "I want people to stop asking themselves, what's the new *Strictly*? And instead start asking – what's the new *destination content experience* people will love at Saturday tea time?

For a while, we nicknamed it 'The Jackdaw Project' but soon enough it became *The Visionary Leadership Programme*. Top creatives, no more than ten at a time, were put through a gruelling three day bootcamp where no agenda was provided, a mini bus motored them to mystery locations, and they got to hear from some of the most inspiring creative risk takers working in digital, content and business. James Bond producers at Pinewood, indie visionaries, world famous names keen to share their experiences and their expertise.

Lost *Mad Men*

Each cohort was made up of people from all over the creative output areas in Vision – from comedy and drama to the Natural History Unit. We wanted to see what could happen if we brought people together in a high pressure environment and encouraged them to think cross-genre, transmedia, new, different.

Some of the ideas born in the Visionary Leadership Programme made it on air. But not enough. One of my favourite contributors was the founder of Kudos (the indie that made *Spooks* at the time), Stephen Garrett. He shared the highlights of his Oxford lecture series which unpicked the 2010 series *Lost* and revealed the power of creating without boundaries.

He showed how the show spilled out of the TV into the real world, criss-crossing through digital and analogue and turning characters into people and a viewership into a cult follow-ship. "And if you don't start *thinking* like that, *creating* like that, *producing* like that... the younger generations you're already losing will be... *lost*."

His thesis was that you have to do something bold, brilliant and *relevant* to differentiate and attract younger audiences. One of his anecdotes was about a fan who started a fake Twitter account pretending to be a character from *Mad Men* – Betty Draper, the beleaguered wife of advertising mogul Don Draper.

The producers had the confidence and the chutzpah to start pointing to it, and using it in promotions. Suddenly, Betty was spirited into the present, we were getting to know her through the power of digital. She had a voice, she was real, she was alive. We could peek into her life through a digital peephole.

She breathed life and excitement into another dimension to give fans of the show another layer of involvement.

Time travel

Disintermediation allows you to float through multiple dimensions of time and space. A bit like a Tardis – the internet is way bigger on the inside than it is on the outside…. And just like the Tardis, it can whisk you through Time And Relative Dimension In Space…

If we scoot through the internet, there is a free world of stuff to inform, educate and entertain. Oh wait…

"*And whereas in view of the widespread interest which is taken by Our People in services which provide audio and visual material by means of broadcasting, the internet or the use of newer technologies, and of the great value of such services as means of disseminating information, education and entertainment, We believe it to be in the interests of Our People that there should continue to be an independent corporation and that it should provide such services, and be permitted to engage in other compatible activities within a suitable legal framework.*"

This is an extract from the Royal Charter "*for the continuance of the British Broadcasting Corporation*" dated 2016. The *disintermediation* meeting we had forecasting 'the world in 2016' was in the run-up to this. But in the Royal Charter, there is only one mention of the word children and one mention of the word teenagers, and I could not find any mention of the word young.

Death of the schedule

The BBC's first Director-General, Lord Reith, was an engineer. He wanted the BBC to '*bring the best of everything to the greatest number of homes*'. In a disintermediated world, that means making your content available to as many people as possible through as many means as possible. It's about making connections.

These days, we have the death of the schedule. People watch what they want, when they want. They listen to what they want, when they want. They download what they want, when they want.

We think about relationships with audiences in completely different ways. I was a TV producer for a very long time, proud to have been both Programme Editor on *Breakfast with Frost* and for a while, the BBC's Election Results Editor. I made programmes on palaeontology featuring Sir David Attenborough. I previously worked at both Sky and ITN.

"Audiences are at the heart of everything we do".

When you are a TV producer, your job is to relentlessly try to serve your audiences. You should think about who they are, what they care about, what they do, how they live. You have to try to make content they'll love, find informative, educational, entertaining.

Towards the end of my time as a TV producer, we were just edging into social media. I remember setting up a MySpace profile for one of my projects, and dabbling a little in the video game world of Second Life.

Before that, people used to write in to the programmes. You'd get piles of correspondence every week, and you would need to do your best to get back to everyone. That was the nearest thing you had back then to a more conversational relationship with your audience. We were still – literally – *broad*casting. But safely.

The Man with the Flower in his Mouth

Which brings me back to the Tardis. If we travel back in time to 1930, we would – completely counterintuitively – visit a bolder, more audacious BBC. Prepared to experiment. Prepared to fail. Under the watchful gaze of its engineer DG, it made its first ever TV drama. Just eight years after starting life in The Strand in the old Marconi building.

They broadcast an English translation of an Italian play: *The Man with the Flower in his Mouth*. I urge you to Google it and watch it on YouTube. You will be as astonished as I was when I first stumbled upon it.

It's not just the risk-taking, the storytelling, or the innovation that captures the imagination. It's the daring of presenting something as surreal and as extraordinary as this to the nation.

"The man with the flower in his mouth," intones the narrator, with clipped, precise, beautiful pronunciation, "is seated at one of the tables." At this stage, we do not see the man, but we are hearing the whistling of a train, and feeling the judder of the engine on the tracks as we are transported to a railway café. He goes on "...silently observing the customer, who, at a neighbouring table, is sipping a mint frappé through a straw." It's a story of existentialism. The meaning of life. Relevancy.

It was watched by the Prime Minister of the day, Ramsay MacDonald. The engineer John Logie Baird had installed one of his prototype 'televisors' into Downing Street. In those days, it was almost unimaginable that you could view *people on a screen* in your living room.

Time travel back to today, and we can view *people on a screen* in a multitude of ways. Children and teenagers rarely sit down in the living room with their families to watch the 'televisor'. Which was why the BBC took the bold and brave decision to move the BBC Three TV channel for young people to a purely online proposition in 2016. And why Radio 1 for years has been more about live music events and other content streams than 'just' radio.

And why CBBC and CBeebies moved away from the flagship BBC One and secondary BBC Two channels as part of the digital switchover to online channels.... although this strategy flip-flops over time, as indeed might the BBC Three strategy.

As I was writing this chapter I heard that the youth channel might be heading back to television.

Hand on heart, I love the BBC. It's part of the fabric of our nation. Like the Queen and BT, it's been in my life as long as I can remember. I grew up with *Blue Peter* and *Newsround*, *Multi-coloured Swapshop* and *Tomorrow's World*. The things I used to love, back then, most likely wouldn't work for today's audiences. But stories transcend time and space. As Doctor Who knows only too well…

"Hey, do you mind if I tell you a story? One you might not have heard. All the elements in your body were forged many, many millions of years ago in the heart of a faraway star that exploded and died. That explosion scattered those elements across the desolations of deep space. After so, so many millions of years these elements came together to form new stars and new planets… Until, eventually, they came together to make you. You are unique in the universe. There is only one [you], and there will never be another."

Today, we are in The Future, and broadcasting has scattered into a disintermediated world of microcasts, podcasts and multicasts. We don't want the star of the BBC to explode and die. But it needs to crack follow-ship. It needs to tell stories. Big data and AI can help determine behavioural insights, but they can't touch your heart, delight you, or move you.

There is only one BBC, and there will never be another. It needs to work out how, in this disintermediated world, it can "bring the best of everything to the greatest number of homes". Form new stars, and new planets. Let's hope it does.

About the writer

Kerensa Jennings is BT Group Director of Digital Impact. She leads a large portfolio of social impact programmes and initiatives. Previously she was CEO of the Inspiring Digital

Enterprise Award (iDEA), an international programme aiming to help address the digital skills gap.

Earlier in her career, Kerensa was a TV producer and the BBC's Head of Strategic Delivery. Her work on the BBC's Make it Digital strategy earned the Innovation Enterprise Chief Strategy Officer's Best Innovation Award. She is also a visiting professor at the University of Huddersfield, an executive coach and a bestselling author. She is passionate about helping people unlock their potential and has been selected among the most influential women in UK tech for the last four years by *Computer Weekly*.

Vox Populi

Francesca Clayton, 28, teacher, Leicestershire

First choice for me in the day is Zoe Ball on Radio 2, which I listen to on my way to work, then I use the iPlayer. I hardly ever access the BBC on television as I don't have a TV aerial. Louis Theroux is also superb, I watch all his programmes. Not having a TV aerial, it is helpful having the iPlayer and the option to watch live.

I'm getting to realise how biased the BBC's media is, which has put me off watching the news. It's the worst thing about the BBC. As a teacher, I found it very unsupportive when schools were opening. It had been so vocal about the importance of lockdown, but instantly changed to how schools must open and teachers are preventing this, describing us a lazy and just wanting more holidays.

If the BBC didn't exist, I'd really miss Animal Park and some of the older shows from BBC Three that aren't on other platforms.

The licence fee has to change, it's not value for money – we only pay it because it's the law. The other platforms and services don't require it – we prefer to pay subscription or get content for free. We mainly watch Netflix which has a lot of the BBC content.

Chapter 7

Living with the enemy

There are many small wins possible for the BBC, as it now seeks to improve engagement with younger audiences. However, the wider competitive landscape has changed beyond recognition in the last decade. All stakeholders should understand that and set expectations appropriately. Otherwise disappointment beckons, says Alex DeGroote

> *'If you know the enemy and know yourself, you need not fear the result of a hundred battles. If you know yourself but not the enemy, for every victory gained you will also suffer a defeat'.*

Sun-Tzu's hard-bitten war proverb may not at first glance seem appropriate for the challenge which faces the BBC right now over the 'lost generation'. However, if we substitute the word 'enemy' for 'media' it may make more sense.

I personally approach the BBC 'lost generation' conundrum with two hats on: firstly as a professional media analyst, investor and corporate adviser of 20 years' standing; and secondly as a father of young-ish sons born in 2007 and 2011 respectively, who inform my understanding of what the BBC means to their generation, and how they spend their precious leisure time.

If the BBC does nothing else, I would ask it to double-down in its market research with these younger age groups. They know the enemy better than anyone, and love it – whether that's

Xbox gaming, Netflix or YouTube vloggers on the iPad you have never heard of. For what it's worth my own children's strongest affinity with the BBC at present (during the lockdown) is through Bitesize and a handful of programmes, including Strictly and Dad's Army.

The struggle to adapt

On close examination, my view is that the BBC's current malaise with younger viewers and listeners reflects a struggle to adapt at speed to a mixed-economy approach over the last decade. It is also falling victim to rapidly changing technology, consumption patterns and business models, which have emerged in media over that same period. Most of these external changes are global and totally beyond the BBC's control.

At the same time in the areas of content and user experience (UX) – to name just two domains – it does feel to me that the BBC has been introspective, if not hermetically sealed. Just as the wider media ecosystem has been increasingly governed by new forms of content, and browsing and interoperability. Particularly, in terms of youth consumption patterns.

Why, however, is that last decade so important? What altered? It is in that 2010-2019 period that media changed forever – in terms of the internet, social platforms, smartphones, other enabled devices, household broadband, user-generated content, gaming, video, streaming – with implications for the UK incumbents, such as the BBC, the other public service broadcasters (PSBs) and even multichannel pay TV companies such as Sky.

That decade also saw the unstoppable emergence of FAAMNG – the grouping of Facebook, Apple, Amazon, Microsoft, Netflix and Google (or Alphabet). As I write the economic might of FAAMNG accounts for 25 per cent of the entire US stock market. This cohort of big tech companies, all domiciled in US, now also frames the media rulebook' in a way which was unimaginable at the start of the decade.

To give one example, content production budgets (mainly scripted drama) have ballooned over the last decade. Netflix, c$15bn pa; Amazon Prime, c$7bn pa; Apple TV, c$6bn pa. compared to £1.6bn annually for BBC television. There is an abundance of over-the-top (OTT) platforms all vying for consumers in the attention economy. This high-end boxset drama is now paid for by monthly consumer subscriptions, not advertising and certainly not the licence fee.

The cost of production is increasing. On one hand, the BBC cannot compete on like-for-like terms with these FAAMNG behemoths. On the other hand, nor should it expect to.

Mainstream subscription video on demand (SVOD) does not play in the news or current affairs space, for example, and so the BBC and PSBs are unconstrained here. Nor is FAAMNG always the enemy in a commercial sense. They offer huge co-production opportunities.

The long and short of it

Whilst long-form drama can pull in serious SVOD audiences, the fact also remains that average attention span of a millennial is less than 20 seconds. Short-form videos fit their lifestyles and social media habits. Platforms like WhatsApp, TikTok and Snapchat are hugely popular amongst millennials, Gen Z and even younger age groups. How is the BBC relevant in this part of the sector, including user generated content?

The current problem of being relevant to younger audiences in particular is common across all PSBs, not just the BBC. Viewing time to PSB channels by 16-24 year age groups declined by 38 per cent between 2014 and 2018, to just 38 minutes daily. Over the same period, SVOD consumption doubled amongst this cohort, to 52 minutes daily.

More time is spent watching content online, than live broadcast TV. Ironically BBC content itself is consumed more widely on non-BBC SVOD platforms than BBC's own on demand platforms. It is surely absurd that BBC programmes are watched more regularly on Netflix than iPlayer (4.7 minutes per day of BBC content on SVOD compared to 2.5 minutes per day on BBC iPlayer for 16-34 year olds).

Additionally, the growth of non-licensable media content is increasingly posing a specific challenge to the BBC. This includes, for example, user-generated or 'amateur' programmes online (e.g. live transmissions using Periscope, Facebook Live, YouTube live streaming or company-sponsored websites), as well as non-BBC catch-up including ITV Hub and Channel 4's on-demand All4.

This is relevant because the BBC licence fee accounts for c75 per cent of the BBC's near £5bn revenue, with the remaining 25 per cent from commercial activities. Declining levels of licence fee take-up may be accelerated if decriminalisation becomes law.

YouTube itself is in many ways the poster child for the lost generation in the UK. The audience stats, sourced from Ofcom, are highly revealing. The 16-24 age group spend 73 minutes a day viewing content, dropping to 34 minutes a day for all citizens. The range of content is widespread from music video to vlogging to gaming to original PSB content. Short-form content is, of course, de rigueur.

Ofcom's own (latest available) 2018 audience data tells us that the average UK citizen enjoyed two hours and 33 minutes of BBC content daily across all platforms. Citizens in the age group 16-34 years enjoyed one hour and 17 minutes. Consumption in the younger age group is 50 per cent of the entire population.

Based on the latest data, the rate of total consumption decline across these two cohorts (all ages, and 16-34 years) was 10 minutes and five minutes per annum respectively. Hence, if we were to extrapolate this trend for say five years from 2018 onwards, on a straight-line basis, the average UK citizen would be well below two hours of BBC daily. And the younger age group well below one hour. BBC reach can remain impressive, but frequency is undoubtedly in decline.

No lack of innovation

Make no mistake, the BBC has been innovative in recent years. BBC Sounds was launched with an aim of attracting a younger audience to live and on-demand radio as well as podcasts. This appears to be working. Radio, perhaps surprisingly, outpaces live TV in terms of consumption minutes for everyone. Content is now also available on the BBC iPlayer for longer, which is an under-utilised asset.

At the same time, there is a limit to what the BBC can achieve. This is the time of Covid-19. The BBC's resource constrained. In its own words: 'Since 2010, when the licence fee was frozen and the BBC was required to take on responsibility for funding the World Service, subsidising rural broadband and supporting S4C and local television, the funding for services for UK audiences has fallen in real terms by 18 per cent'.

The BBC's retiring Director-General, Lord Hall, has championed Director of Content, Charlotte Moore and, of course, the challenge awaits her in terms of finding winning content for younger audiences. Establishing winning production formulas remains however that elusive combination of perspiration and inspiration.

So where can the BBC further revise its services? There are many small wins possible for the BBC, in my view. To adapt to changing viewing behaviours and improve 'attention share' of younger age groups it should:

- **examine seamless distribution to all ages**. There is a channel gap between CBBC (< 11 years) and BBC Three

(>16 years). BBC iPlayer is now trying to fill the void more clearly, but the execution can be further improved.

- **embrace short-form content**. Social media platforms are not the only players in short-form content. Former Disney and DreamWorks CEO Jeffrey Katzenberg has cofounded Quibi, a dedicated short-form SVOD content service – more competition for the BBC in its target youth segments. It remains to be seen if Quibi can convert long-form premium film and TV fans into short-form subscribers, but the BBC needs a more identifiable strategy here.

- **not ignore the archive value 'in search of the new'.** Many new BBC content initiatives will look to narrow target demographics, say 12-15 age groups specifically. However, this ignores the broad content appeal of programmes such as *Strictly, Would I Lie to You* and *The Apprentice.*

- **develop further social media linkage**. By now, any user of social media understands the principle of newsfeeds, 'likes' and sharing. What I would like to see is the BBC incorporate more external sources and feeds into its own-site content. More links, more references which in turn leads to more 'virality'.

- **improve marketing**. Amongst younger age groups, the BBC brand is arguably less well known than Netflix and YouTube. The BBC spends much less on external branding than other broadcasters and historically has relied on promotion through owned media channels. Social media advertising is how to drive more youth traffic.

- **be clear on SVOD.** About half of all UK households have at least one SVOD subscription, with an even higher take-up rate amongst younger households. But what is the BBC actually hoping to achieve through Britbox, its joint venture with ITV? Especially with question marks over long-term funding. Knowledge and data on what the audience is prepared to pay for perhaps?

- **develop iPlayer**. With the time extension of programme availability now effective, iPlayer has been at last set free. UX is good. Improved functionality, curation and personalisation will underline the value of iPlayer, which perhaps has not been fully grasped yet by the Netflix-conscious younger age groups. This move from primarily being a catch-up service to a streaming service will be a test of strategy and execution.
- **build on the relaunch of Bitesize**. This is a trusted education site already and helps individual students deliver on learning potential, as well as broadening support for the 16+ audience, and those looking to develop life skills. This also conforms to the original aims and objectives of the BBC.
- **value BBC News Online**: This is the leading online news brand in the UK. The website is more than 20 years old. It has huge global reach, c65m unique browsers each week. But it can be scaled intelligently using social media platforms (e.g. Instagram and YouTube) to reach younger audiences.
- **win the Covid-19 war.** Finally, Covid-19 is sure to prove disruptive to BBC on so many levels. But a laudable objective is set out to 'own' coverage of this pandemic with accurate and incisive reporting. It may prove the defining news event of this decade and the BBC can regain interest of the younger audiences, across platforms, with lifetime benefits.

About the writer

Alex DeGroote is a former highly rated sell-side media and internet sector analyst. He worked in equity capital markets for European investment banks such as Credit Agricole, Panmure Gordon and Peel Hunt between 1997-2018. He is now an adviser to a number of boutique finance firms including

Trillium Partners and Radnor Capital and is an adviser to a number of start-ups in the media, tech and related sectors. He contributes to publications such as *Digiday, The Guardian, Campaign* and Bloomberg.

Sound bite #4

Keith Brown MSP, deputy leader of the Scottish National Party

Many younger people don't use the BBC as they don't see it as relevant to their lives.

Young people are creating digital media for now and for the future – and the BBC is in danger of being left behind.

Despite a few notable exceptions the vast majority of resources and spend for news and in TV drama and programme making, it is geared towards a much older audience.

The situation is magnified in Scotland. The BBC has had three decades to make sure it takes account of devolution, but it still struggles and too much of the output remains rooted in London.

Full autonomy of broadcasting powers in the devolved nations is needed. Only by loosening the metropolitan grip and enabling greater creativity through local autonomy will the BBC be able to attract back younger audiences.

Chapter 8

Gen Z – public service TV's lost generation

Technology has granted the audience unprecedented control over and access to the content it views. This has caused a huge change in who creates content, how that content is produced, how stories are told and the way they are consumed. The biggest impact has been to those born after 2001 – the so-called Generation Z; and as the next consumer generation they are critical to the future economics of the media landscape. We are bombarded with statistics telling us that linear TV has lost that audience. Claire Hungate asks why is that loss so stark and whether linear can win them back?

My twins are four years old and until (very) recently they thought the television set was called CBeebies; now that's what I call brand (dis-)attribution. So how is it that the BBC can entirely lose that audience when they are old enough to discover Superheroes and Disney – and not win them back until they are 50+?

What has caused the seismic movements to the broadcast landscape over the last number of years and how did the BBC (and UK linear broadcasters generally) miss the memo?

Is it technology, or is it content – is content still king or has distribution taken the crown? And has linear TV's denial of the power of audience been its downfall?

I spent 18 years in TV production; helping grow 'super indie' Shed Media and then selling it to Warner Bros, then an entrepreneurial studio grown from creativity – now Warner Media, owned by a telecoms company.

The global media market and the economics that drive it have been changing rapidly; the highly leveraged titans of global media, such as Apple, Comcast, Disney, AT&T, Netflix and the not-so-highly-leveraged Amazon will battle it out to be the winner of the eyeballs. The UK domestic public service broadcast (PSB) market has limped to keep pace with this change.

In 2017 I transitioned into the world of digital – of social media and social video content – and it became obvious that the driving force in the evolution of content wasn't broadcasters – it was the audience.

Social media studios understand audience because their lives revolve around them; audience is everything – audience engagement, interaction, appreciation – you can see it all in real time; it looms large. And it is what motivates everything you do; every post, every piece of content, every comment, when you post, what you post, if you post. If something doesn't drive audience engagement – you take it down – immediately. But it's about watching audience reaction in real time and reacting to that audience reaction.

In this regard particularly, I think 'old media' can learn a lot from the new.

A new in which audiences congregate around passion points, both passionate niches (think Esports) and global consumer brands (think *Friends*); a new in which audiences want to be part of a community which social media allows, a new in which an ability to tap into culture in an authentic way, can garner real brand loyalty. Netflix gets this…it seeks to make niches global, super serving audiences content to build viewer engagement, stickiness and brand attribution.

Sadly for me, as someone who has spent most of my career in content production, I actually think it's technology, rather than content, that is the great enabler amid all this movement – the conduit to giving the audience the expectation of content, anywhere, always, on demand. Content comes a close second; great content can still cut through but it requires equally great distribution and accessibility to do so. And where Netflix has the commercial freedom and audacity to experiment with content and distribution, the UK PSBs have not.

Technology and its evolution has shaped a generation and that generation is now the emergent consumer group driving the media economy.

What is Generation Z?

According to Bloomberg, using United Nations data, almost a third of the world's population is Generation Z – that is – born around 2001 or later:

- that's the year Al Qaeda launched an attack on the Twin Towers;
- the year the first *Harry Potter*, *Lord of the Rings* and *Shrek* films were released and Britney and Justin donned their iconic coordinating denim outfits for the American Music Awards;
- and in technology: Wikipedia went on-line and the first iPod was released.

A year later wireless headphones hit the streets, followed by camera phones and smart phones; YouTube in 2005; Apple TV in 2007; Hulu in 2008; and by the time Gen Z was ten it could watch content on an iPad or a smart TV – the perfect groundwork laid for it to stream Netflix in 2010.

Gen Z is coming of age and now comprises 20 per cent of the global workforce; its members can vote and are dominating the consumer landscape.

How can broadcasters and content producers engage, entertain and market to a generation born with smart phones in its hands, which has an intuitive connection to technology, which is used to consuming content and stories in an entirely different way than we are used to distributing or telling them – a generation which doesn't remember a world without Netflix, Amazon, Apple, YouTube and Facebook or smart TVs and phones. A generation which demands choice, value for money, great technology and content everywhere, whenever it wants it.

So what do we know about this Generation Z, described below by a 2019 Snapchat report:

"They're the hyper-connected, highly opinionated generation, moved to activism as the internet and social media landscape has made them acutely conscious of and concerned about world events. Having lived in an era of overall progress when it comes to issues like marriage equality and body positivity, they're forging new territory in broader conversations about identity; this is the cohort of gender fluidity, diversity and inclusivity in all its forms."

Its members are digital natives and content consumption is a lifestyle for them.

- They are technology reliant.
- They are multi taskers and could be using up to five screens at once.
- They were born during a time of heightened global tension with terrorism and Al-Qaeda dominating the news, making them anxious about safety; the Covid-19 pandemic has only furthered this anxiety.
- They were born during recession, which makes them pragmatic about money; this will potentially be exacerbated in the current climate.
- They don't see difference or talk about diversity – they live with it.

- They are health conscious – less likely to smoke or drink – and are happy to socialise online without going to parties.
- But they value their privacy and are aware of data issues online.
- Professionally, they are entrepreneurial and worried about their future and will often have more than one job (the so called 'gig economy').

Smartphone use is pretty much ubiquitous in this generation and about half of them are connected online about ten hours a day. Media consumption for Gen Zs is embedded in their daily lives so they are not even consciously making a decision to co nsume content. Among teens – 13-18-year-olds – smartphones are used almost three hours a day to consume TV shows, videos, music, games and social media.

As for content the good news is that Gen Zs love it. They want as much as they can possibly get – be that creator content on YouTube or TikTok or 236 episodes of 20-year-old sitcom *Friends*. The bad news for linear broadcast networks is that they are tied neither to TV services to watch it nor to a big piece of kit in the living room.

Gen Zs tend to use over-the-top services that are not tied to TV services. They do watch TV, but are more likely to consume content on Netflix and YouTube.

According to 59 per cent of Gen Z video consumption is done via over-the-top (OTT) services vs 29 per cent for TV; 70 per cent of Gen Zs watch more than two hours of YouTube each day, as opposed to their predecessors – the Millennials – for whom TV and cable are used together with OTT services for media consumption.

The drivers for consumption by Gen Zs are increasingly shifting as they spend more time on their smart phones engaged in social media apps. For Gen Zs, social media is a major way of engaging with a community, as opposed to being just a digital broadcasting platform. It's also a way to participate – to be part of the conversation; hence the domination of gaming and Esports via sites like Twitch and YouTube.

Netflix invested in Generation Z

And as regards their consumption of media, content is a lifestyle, not just entertainment. It's not their attention spans that are short – it's their interest span; their bullshit detector is highly developed and they can easily sniff out content produced by those who aren't genuinely tapped into their culture or that doesn't feel authentic. Getting traditional TV producers to produce content for digital platforms for a Gen Z audience simply does not cut it – the way stories are told and consumed – the beats of a story – are different.

For those seeking to attract that audience; they should think about engaging communities around passion points, niches or big consumer brands that they care about – if it disappears from their feed or your service tomorrow – will they notice and if they do – will they care? Even Netflix look for niches and passions to attract audience behind their big tent poles shows. This isn't just about an amorphous age group; within that are 'taste groups' – communities – passion lead niches.

Another interesting contrast between Netflix and the BBC is that, while the BBC was closing BBC Three as a linear channel and halving its budget, Netflix realised that generally, investment in premium content for the under 30s was sparse. Not only did it invest in this demographic – it actively wooed them with marketing campaigns directed at them and by advertising across the platforms they love, in a manner that engaged and appealed.

In the UK certainly, a generation on which the BBC turned its back and withheld their allowance, found a new home – with Netflix, the parents who loved and spoiled them.

Influencers who make their name on social media platforms like Instagram, TikTok, and YouTube are increasingly important drivers of consumption and content itself is adapting accordingly. Whether it's music or video, influencer content is short-form, off-the-cuff, authentic, shareable and highly relatable. This makes it easy for Gen Z fans to consume the content fluidly across multiple channels and devices throughout the day.

Influencers have a strong presence and built-in distribution, but they also have a deeply personal relationship with their fans, which allows them to create storylines they already know will resonate with their audience – they live and die with their audience.

This is a generation which is audience first, digital first, social first, video first.Content is consumed in a seamless and organic way. Businesses in the media and entertainment ecosystem that adapt accordingly will win. Gen Zs are watching TV content and are following TV brands – they just aren't necessarily watching them on scheduled linear TV.

As an industry it was TV's failure to keep track of audiences and effectively communicate with them on their terms and on their preferred digital platforms, that means the PSB broadcasters are so woefully behind the digital disruption that their frenemies at YouTube and Facebook have wreaked since Gen Z entered the world.

And now TikTok, a platform with an almost 70 per cent under 30 demographic and which allows everyone to be an influencer and for their post to effectively reach a large audience (almost impossible now for a new entrant to YouTube for example) is stealing a march on the competition.

Today, six years after moving BBC Three online and slashing its budget, the BBC has re-upped Three's content spend and is talking about moving it back on the box. But why? Isn't that too little too late – isn't that just tokenism?

It might give a bigger platform to content produced for BBC Three – and yes it's true there has been some cut-through content – but will it bring a new Gen Z audience to linear TV or to the BBC's other channels? Will it be powerful enough to make Gen Zs care about the BBC in the same way Baby Boomers care about the BBC? Or would the BBC be better off investing in the content, the marketing and distribution of that content and rethinking the branding around BBC Three?

Would it be better off fighting regulatory, commercial restrictions and attribution issues that prevent it from taking its content and its dialogue with its desired audiences to the platforms where they play; new audiences who will engage with, participate in and care about the future of the BBC – where they can build loyalty and re-engage the attribution instinct that was so strong at the age of four?

In order to survive in a licence fee- (even partially) funded environment, the BBC must harness the power of Generation Z, and Generation Alpha that follows it. We must question whether investing in a new linear TV channel right now is the most effective method of doing that in a world where resources are stretched, consumer choice is huge and only increasing day by day, and the well-funded competition just keeps getting stronger.

About the writer

Claire Hungate is an internationally recognised expert in the media space; her experience spans the financing, production, distribution and commercialisation of audio-visual content across multiple distribution platforms. She has spent the last 20 years in executive roles in the television and digital media sectors, including running some of the biggest and most successful TV production companies in the world including Wall to Wall, Shed Media and Warner Bros. TV UK.

Claire is a board member at Media Capital Technologies, a global entertainment company which funds premium content;

advisor to the board at Chimp Productions, Richard Hammond's (*Grand Tour*, *Top Gear*) content production company and chair of, and an investor in, The Nerve Media Group, an online music library aimed at the TV production sector. In 2019 she was chair of the content steering committee of the International Broadcasting Conference and is a well-respected speaker on the international conference circuit. Twitter @ClaireHungate

https://www.linkedin.com/in/clairehungate/.

Sound bite #5

Chris Matheson MP for the City of Chester. Shadow Minister of State for Media

The BBC has an obligation to universality, which doesn't mean every programme must appeal to everyone, but that there must be something for as many sections of society as possible; reflecting diversity of background and experience.

'Youth' programming is nothing new, whether on the BBC or any channel. But how younger audiences access content might be different.

To be fair to the BBC, they led the way in streaming with iPlayer, and with BBC Sounds have sharpened up audio and digital content delivery into an accessible streaming service.

Of course delivery has changed completely in the last 15 years: most young people have their own smartphone or tablet so there is more demand for shorter, bite-sized content to fit that delivery mechanism in a way that each generation is most comfortable with.

Yet that content still has to be produced, and the funding structure for the BBC gives a stable foundation not just to the BBC but to the wider broadcasting ecosystem, while ensuring that the younger generation can access home grown content.

Critically, the BBC provides the reliable, impartial and trustworthy source of news and information for young people, which at the very least can act as a reference point of stability to return to in a world of fake news, hyperbole and disinformation.

Whether it was John Craven's Newsround 40 years ago, or Radzi Chinyangana's recent work for World Service TV the BBC's core mission is to help younger audiences develop and seek out the truth from the fake news.

Chapter 9

Did the 1960s' pop pirates show the way?

The BBC's pop music network, Radio 1, has been highly successful in reaching young audiences over many decades. Paul Robinson asks what the corporation can learn from radio to help it re-attract this hard-to-reach target audience that no longer loves it as much as previous generations

When BBC Radio 1 burst onto the air in September 1967 it wasn't just to replace the much-loved and extensively-listened-to pirate radio stations made illegal by the then Labour government's Marine Offences Act, but an attempt to appeal to young audiences.

The BBC didn't get it entirely right at the start. Sitting uncomfortably alongside Tony Blackburn and Emperor Rosko, whose lunchtime show incidentally had the quaint title of *Midday Spin*, was Wally Whyton's *Country meets Folk* and Michael Aspel's *Family Favourites*.

The corporation was certainly in two minds about its new 'pop music' network and it even had Radio 1 located in a separate building linked by an underground tunnel to Broadcasting House. You wouldn't want Radio 4's Jack De Manio, the revered Today presenter and former World War II soldier, bumping into Kenny Everett in the corridors.

Radio 1's home of Egton House served it well and lasted nearly 50 years until the recent reorganisation of Broadcasting House in which it was absorbed into BH, and then, in homage to one of the network's greatest DJs, named the Peel wing, which sounds more like a hospital than a place to make cool radio for young audiences.

I didn't arrive at Radio 1, initially as Editor and Head of Daytime programmes until 1990, but it was very clear even then, that although Radio 1 was part of the BBC, it sort of wasn't, and in many ways didn't want to be. We were pretty much self-contained in Egton House and we were blessed to have the studios, and the production offices and management all in one building.

It felt like a radio station, and encouraged by the Controller, Johnny Beerling it was a creative, fun and extremely vibrant place to work. Johnny had started at the BBC like so many, as a technical operator, and then studio manager before moving up to produce shows for the BBC Light Programme.

But he had a vision and determination that the BBC had to provide a legal version of the pirates. Probably more than any other Radio 1 Controller Johnny understood how to attract audiences and to foster a creative environment. For many he *was* Radio 1 and much of the network's success is ultimately his.

The anathema of the BBC name

So, whilst working at Radio 1, was a huge thrill and exciting every day, having arrived from commercial radio where I was Programme Controller of the Chiltern Radio Network of stations, it was obvious from the start that Johnny was skilfully managing Radio 1's success with its audience and being part of the Beeb.

I do recall, soon after I started, attending a production meeting discussing the use of the name BBC on air, and being informed that it wasn't smart to brand Radio 1 on air too noticeably as BBC, because it would be anathema to young audiences and they would switch off. My point was how would licence fee payers know that Radio 1 was paid for by them, but that point didn't get much traction in that particular meeting. I asked for, and never saw any research to back up this hypothesis, but it was certainly a mantra on air.

There was a glaring schizophrenia between serving the listeners and the conservatism and bureaucracy in the corporation. This became more acute when John Birt replaced Michael Checkland as Director-General. Checkland was a traditional 'civil service, gentlemanly figure' and Birt a highly intellectual, bright and thrusting former ITV executive. Birt's legacy to the BBC was the far-sighted and rigorous digital strategy, which served it well for many years after his departure, but it was obvious that Radio 1 was sailing into choppy waters.

I am not a fan of Smashy and Nicey, the affectionate but inaccurate portrayal of Radio 1 DJs by Paul Whitehouse and Harry Enfield. You could argue perhaps that some presenters stayed too long and should perhaps have migrated to Radio 2, although the Radio 2 of the early 1990s was not a good fit because its audience profile was then 50+ and its music policy still rooted in the 1960s Light Programme. So these hugely successful and popular DJs had nowhere to go in the BBC.

The Radio 1 of the last 20 years has made much of its goal to have a younger audience and reach specifically the 15-24 age group. Aside from the fact that the overall number of listeners to Radio 1 is now half what it was in the early 1900s, it is also the case that they are much less loyal, listening for fewer hours.

This is to some extent a function of increased competition – Capital, Kiss and other commercial stations are suffering from the same loss of hours listened per listener – but also the universal ownership, at an increasingly young age, of connected, portable devices and some poor editorial decision-making by BBC managers.

However, it is also critical to point out that Johnny Beerling's Radio 1 had a much higher percentage reach and larger absolute numbers of 15-24s listening than the more recent 'youth' incarnations of Radio 1.

You could perhaps argue that Radio 1 then was less a young person's station. Its success and appeal was so great that many 40-year-olds and older were still loyal listeners because they had grown up with Radio 1 in the 1960s and 1970s and didn't want to admit they were no longer young. The same phenomenon of audience targeting was one of the counter intuitive truisms of national newspapers. For many years *The Sun* had a larger number of ABC1 (upmarket) readers than *The Times* because *The Sun* had a much larger overall total circulation than *The Times*.

Another example of this is the Radio 1 Roadshow and its replacement the Radio 1 Big Weekend. The former, which started in July 1973 and had Newquay as its first location, lasted more than 25 years and comprised eight weeks of daily UK holiday location broadcasts. It reached between half and a million people a year who attended in person and many more millions on air. The Big Weekends, a two-day event, is closer to a mini music festival with an emphasis on new music and an attendance of around 20,000 people. The two events are editorially different.

The Roadshow was largely personal appearances by bands, and games with a Radio 1 DJ playing records, in comparison to the live music festival style of the Big Weekend. The latter is clearly 'cooler', more defendable as being public service (a free festival for young people promoting new music) than the Roadshow, which was pure entertainment and that was free for holidaymakers.

However, the critical question is which of the two reached the most young people, and which inspired a strong connection to the BBC and advocacy for it, with the concomitant halo for the licence fee?

The answer is obvious – it was the Radio 1 Roadshow that attracted the most 15-24s. Yes, it also attracted a broader audience, but as a promotional vehicle, it was a juggernaut for BBC Radio 1, and one which the commercial radio stations feared. I recall a Radio 1 Roadshow in Derby, which attracted 40,000 people, and the local independent station couldn't avoid talking about the travel disruption on air caused by its arch rival's presence on its patch.

The BBC unfortunately dug itself into a hole believing that a promotional outside broadcast event that was part of Radio 1's DNA was past its sell by date and canned it. Since then neither Radio 1 nor any BBC radio network has got anywhere near the promotional, brand and editorial effectiveness of the Radio 1 Roadshow.

A misplaced strategy

The commercial radio networks have stolen Radio 1's clothes. Capital's Summertime Ball and Jingle Bell Christmas Ball, originally set up for the London only station, have now become premier events and sell out in hours, attracting much bigger crowds than anything Radio 1 puts on.

The BBC local radio strategy for young people is also curiously misplaced.

Most of the BBC local stations in England since 2019 have introduced minority and youth programming in the evenings. The quality is patchy. I have heard some good new talent, but also some utterly creatively bankrupt content that should never have gone to air.

But, worse, why would a young person turn to their local BBC Radio station for an evening programme? And whilst the most recent Radio 1 Big Weekend was virtual due to Covid-19 lockdown restrictions, all 39 BBC local stations broadcast from the event which the BBC hailed as something only the BBC could do. Yes, that might be true, but being able to do it didn't mean the strategy was right. I suspect the impact on the BBC's 15-24 audience of this initiative was next to zero.

So, what does this tell us about how the BBC should go about attracting this audience?

Firstly, the behaviour of young audiences during the UK lockdown demonstrates that in a crisis, even 15-24s have a tendency to go back to the BBC; early data suggests that trust in public service broadcasting has increased during this period and trust in social media has dropped.

Further, while young people have watched streamed VOD services more during the lockdown, they have also watched the BBC more. And this viewing doesn't appear to be to 'youth-oriented' programming but to mainstream news and entertainment output. The decision by the BBC to drop BBC Three as a broadcast channel, replacing it as an online service, caused a dramatic drop in audience engagement and viewing numbers. The outcome was to reduce the amount of time spent with the BBC by young audiences.

Attempts by the BBC to commission comedy and entertainment programs targeted at 15-24s, such as *Ru Paul's Drag Race* have been undertaken with good intent. However, the lesson learned is that distributing them on third-party platforms, such as social media, online or the BBC iPlayer is not yet a potent enough distribution strategy. The BBC has trialled putting BBC Three on BBC One, but the audiences have not been huge. Perhaps scheduling such programs in peak on BBC One might produce a larger audience.

All the evidence from Radio 1 is that to engage 15-24s it is essential to engage them with compelling entertainment, and that niche or 'youth'-oriented programmes deliver neither the numbers nor the positive approbation.

Young audiences are known to be less willing to pay the licence fee and that propensity to be perfectly satisfied without

BBC content will be exacerbated if non-payment becomes a civil not a criminal offence.

To keep young people as willing licence-fee payers both now and when they become older will only happen if the BBC becomes a daily habit. That requires the BBC to be relevant to this audience.

To achieve that the BBC strategy should be to serve young people in the round as part of mainstream audiences and not to treat them as a minority. It is also essential to deliver content and BBC experiences that are not only innovative and creatively excellent, but on both minority platforms where young audiences spend time and on mainstream mass audience channels and platforms.

And, finally, maybe there is a lesson from the 1960s pop pirates? A little more risk and daring might go a long way. After all, at least some of the attraction of those stations was that they were not from the BBC?

About the writer

Paul Robinson is a former Managing Editor of BBC Radio 1, and Head of Strategy, BBC Radio and former Managing Director of commercial network Talk Radio.

He was Senior Vice President of Disney Channel Worldwide and Head of Children's content strategy worldwide for Disney, based in Los Angeles and London; he was also CEO of NBC Universal joint venture kids' network and VOD service KidsCo.

He has degrees from Cambridge and Manchester Universities and an MBA from the University of Bradford. He is a multiple award winner and regular speaker and broadcaster.

Sound bite #6

Kirsten O'Brien, presenter, CBBC 1996-99; *SMart*, 1999-2009

Attracting the younger audience is so important because their viewing habits have changed from the traditional linear way of watching television.

It's important that the BBC finds ways to attract and interact with them going forwards that isn't sitting down in front of a television and watching output in a real-time schedule on a channel.

The younger audience wants more control over what they watch and when, they often want access to whole series at once at a time they choose.

They watch on devices; they like to share conten; and they often like short bursts of content. All of this challenges traditional programme making for the BBC.

In terms of attracting this audience I think the BBC partly needs to continue to focus on what it does best, in particular strong children's programming.

It has felt like the tendency has been to see this as low budget in terms of programme funding, but actually it's an area which parents, myself included, hold in high regard and at an early age it's the parents who have control over what children watch.

I think if the BBC can attract audience at an early age this will start to foster their relationship with the brand. But the BBC needs to look at how young people come to content and how long for.

I also think the BBC must continue to fund non-linear output like the recent BBC Bitesize which young people may arrive at but can be a jumping off point for leading to other content within the BBC.

Chapter 10

No hesitation, repetition or deviation

After years of risking irrelevance, there are encouraging signs the BBC is finding ways to re-engage young adults, says Graeme Thompson

As a sixth former at Boldon Comprehensive School on Tyneside in the 1970s I used to walk home for lunch – a round trip of 40 minutes. It wasn't because the food in the school canteen was particularly terrible, it was about getting home in time to listen to the lunchtime output of BBC Radio 4 on the kitchen radio. Feels geeky to admit that now, but that's how it was in the days before multi-channel, multi-platform entertainment.

Typically, I used to catch the last ten minutes of the consumer magazine *You & Yours* and the first ten minutes of the *World at One* before heading back to class. But the highlight of my soup or sandwich lunch was always the 12.30pm slot – comedies like *I'm Sorry I Haven't A Clue* with Humphrey Lyttleton, Willie Rushton and Tim Brooke-Taylor and quizzes such as *Top of the Form* with Bob Holness.

Then there was the evergreen *Desert Island Discs* hosted by the mellifluous Roy Plomley. I particularly loved *Just A Minute* with Kenneth Williams, Derek Nimmo and Nicholas Parsons – still do. Listening to panellists try to speak for a minute on a subject without repetition, hesitation or deviation has always been hugely entertaining.

It was my window on the world. It was life beyond our mining community and it ignited my love of journalism, comedy and the BBC. I suspect I wasn't part of Radio 4's target audience but somehow it didn't occur to me that I wasn't welcome. Tim Brooke-Taylor was, relatively speaking, the young upstart on the *I'm Sorry I Haven't A Clue* panel – at the programme's launch in 1972 he was 32. But many of the voices that inspired my future ambitions were comfortably middle aged and shockingly almost all of them were male.

In radio, time moves more slowly and listeners have to conjure their own pictures. It's about the connection between broadcaster and listener. Age feels less relevant. I was however conscious of class. Back then, BBC diversity and inclusion rarely extended beyond the lesser known Oxbridge colleges.

If there were alternative voices breaking through – voices like mine – I wasn't aware of them. Fast forward more than 40 years and the barriers to entering the psyche of young, impressionable audiences have been almost obliterated. The democratisation of content is just one challenge faced by the BBC.

A decade after lapping up corporation content as an ambitious sixth former, I found myself working as a producer for the BBC in London having served my apprenticeship in newspapers and local radio (where I proudly read the news on the hour in my South Shields accent). I was thrilled to be based at Broadcasting House alongside the presenters, producers and writers who'd inspired me.

I worked in the department producing current affairs and magazine programmes for Radio 4 – including *Woman's Hour* and *You & Yours*. Thirty years on and I know the Radio 1 presenter Jordan North is similarly excited to be at that iconic address in Portland Place after graduating in radio at the University of Sunderland.

But anyone who has spent any time in universities over the last decade will recognise that the current generation of students have not been quite as enamoured of the corporation as we were.

An old-fashioned view

Students – especially those studying media subjects such as journalism – have a tendency to regard 'Auntie' as being old-fashioned. Some of her less auspicious moments such as the fallout from Andrew Gilligan's 'dodgy dossier' interview on the *Today* programme in 2003 are studied as textbook case histories in how not to break a story. So too is the corporation's approach to balance in the 2016 Brexit referendum.

I recall University of Sunderland students back then complaining that interviews with expert scientists were being 'balanced' by the opposite argument from people with very different credentials. It felt like a cop out. Students, already acutely aware of the rise of fake news and the manipulation of social media, felt the national broadcaster should have done better.

The trust argument is important. If we accept that most young people are much less Euro-sceptic than the majority of Brexit voters, the BBC's 'constipated' approach to the referendum – as described by the film producer and Labour peer Lord David Puttnam – was a key turning point in the way many viewed the broadcaster.

Puttnam said after the referendum in 2016 that newsrooms and producers had effectively been hamstrung by the strict rules on impartiality which govern the BBC. The obsession with balance, he said, made it hard to distinguish the facts from the fiction.

There are other reasons why students feel equivocal about the broadcaster. The BBC is just another platform. Some students even refer to its mainstream television channel as 115 – its number on the Sky and Freeview electronic programme guides (EPG). Others just call it the iPlayer.

And unlike my younger self back in the '70s, the one thing they're not short of is choice. It's easy to dismiss the proliferation of creators and platforms as merely white noise impeding the discoverability of great content, if only you knew it was there. Names and commercial fortunes are made on YouTube and the idea that everyone waits for the same scheduled programming is now fantasy. This generation has grown up with multi-channel and smart technology and is adept at finding what it wants to hear or watch, when it wants it.

TikTok is the latest social media platform to capture the imagination of Gen Z. It's crammed with memes and body beautiful clips, but in the battle to be found, creators deploy broadcast trickery such as green screens and jump cuts and invest hours in planning seemingly simple vignettes. It's a creative and highly engaging hub. It's where young audiences are.

Like more established social channels, the faces young people see here look much more like their own than they have historically found at the BBC. It may not have been an issue for the 17-year-old me, but it sure is now.

Thankfully for those of us who support the survival of the BBC as a public service broadcaster, young adults do seem to be finding their way back to its portals.

The former *Daily Mirror* journalist and law lecturer Carole Watson observes: "When it comes to news, younger people tend not to switch on TV or radio, but consume their news via social media links to stories that interest them, which leads to all sort of issues regarding gravitas and fact-checking.

"However, since the pandemic, several journalism students have told me they have downloaded the BBC News App to their phones to check on the latest information such as the daily coronavirus figures."

What students have noticed

There's also appreciation among media students of the BBC's role in paying for the introduction of local democracy reporters to work in the newsrooms of struggling provincial newspaper titles. And the corporation's attempts to commission more content from the nations and regions has also been noticed.

Conversely, so has the decision in May 2020 to pull production of factual and current affairs television programmes from the English regions pending a review. Not so in the nations of Scotland, Wales and Northern Ireland where political and factual shows rightly continue to thrive. If the UK's broadcast centres are to go on providing a nursery slope for emerging talent, aspiring media practitioners in England might be forgiven for concluding their prospects might be rosier across the borders.

This increase in the number of younger people making use of the national broadcaster is at the heart of the BBC's Annual Plan published in May 2020. It quotes figures showing that as many as 94 per cent of the UK adult population – and 86 per cent of younger people – have turned to the BBC during the lockdown.

Is it a trend or a blip? Before the virus, Ofcom was reporting that while BBC news has maintained its reputation among most people for trusted and accurate reporting, it is still seen by many as representing a white, middle-class and London-centric point of view not relevant to their lives.

The corporation, and its new director-general Tim Davie, will certainly be hoping 2020 is a turning point. A renewed focus on engaging with the 16-34 age group includes investing more in BBC Three – the online channel which has produced some of the corporation's most popular shows with that elusive cohort.

In April 2020, *Normal People* generated 16.2m requests in just seven days on the BBC iPlayer. Five million of those were from 16-34s contributing to a record-breaking week of 21.8m requests for the service. Other mainstream hits commissioned by BBC Three include *Fleabag* and *Killing Eve*.

It will be interesting to see whether BBC Three reappears as a separate broadcast channel. In an age where content is discoverable to younger people across multiple platforms, it feels counter-intuitive to defer to traditional hierarchies by putting it back on the TV.

There was more encouraging news for the corporation in a Reuters Institute report from September 2019 on Public Service Media in Europe. The study compared how audiences between 18 and 25 use offline and online public service news with the use of their strongest private competitor online and with the use of YouTube and Facebook for news. The figures showed that:

- US-based platforms such as Facebook and YouTube are more widely used as sources of online news by young people than public service media in many European countries. Facebook is more widely named by young audiences as a source of online news than public service media in seven of the eight countries covered and YouTube in six of eight countries covered.
- Despite broadcast public service news being much less widely used among younger audiences, offline still delivers wider reach than online in every case except the BBC.
- In Europe, younger audiences' consistent preference for online news over offline sources, is not the case in the UK. The BBC is alone in the sample in having significantly higher online reach among young audiences than in the wider public. In every other country covered, reach is lower.

A non-scientific poll of undergraduates in Sunderland and Stratford-upon-Avon tended to support the BBC's claim that it is improving its reach in that age group. Some 75 per cent admitted to using the BBC – mostly via the Sounds app, the iPlayer and on catch-up. But almost everyone claimed to make more use of Netflix.

Here are some sample quotes:

> *"I sometimes use iPlayer for dramas and documentaries. I use it mostly to watch sport, live games and MOTD." – Dom (30)*

> *"Don't much like the BBC. It's like the Daily Mail." – Sophie (22)*

> *"I use the iPlayer mainly and every now and then I'll watch the news especially during this pandemic. Most definitely value the use of iPlayer more than anything as I don't watch TV." – Emily (20)*

> *"I think the only thing that could be improved is maybe the fact that we have such a binge culture now, it would probably make the BBC more appealing for younger people if they released most programmes as a whole season at a time on iPlayer." – Alex (19)*

> *"I watch BBC via social media such as Facebook and Twitter. Normally watch catch-up/on demand – never usually live." – Ed (20)*

Perhaps a lesson from these comments is that choice and responsiveness to consumption habits are key. And that means all legacy organisations, not just the BBC, either appropriating disruptive practices or celebrating their differences as an alternative provider.

Inflexibility is not a good look when you are trying to reach young people. Data suggests 85 per cent of video on YouTube is viewed with the sound off – speaking to the contexts of consumption and necessitating subtitling or on-screen graphics. It's just the same as shooting vertical video – for so long a red line for broadcasters, who have finally begun to appreciate that such a change has a profound benefit for millions consuming content on their smartphones.

109

The challenge facing the BBC is that its remit is to appeal to everybody at a time when everybody is goggle-eyed with choice. And if it's to keep its licence fee model of funding, it has to prove itself relevant and robust in the face of political and media interests jealous of its reach. The wit and wisdom of Kenneth Williams and Willie Rushton can no longer be deployed in that particular fight. But it's important that the generation calling the shots in the future identify other standard bearers from their ranks prepared to go into battle for Auntie's channels and platforms – without hesitation, repetition or deviation.

About the writer

Graeme Thompson is Pro-Vice-Chancellor for External Relations at the University of Sunderland. He joined the university in 2009 as Dean of the Faculty of Arts and Creative Industries. His portfolio at the university includes media and communications, marketing, alumni relations and the National Glass Centre. Graeme is a former Head of News and Managing Director at ITV Tyne Tees and spent six years as a producer with BBC radio.

He is chair of the Royal Television Society education committee and writes regularly for *Television* magazine. He also chairs the Sunderland Culture company and the community arts project The Cultural Spring.

Vox Populi

Benj Duncan, 20, student, Newcastle

I don't consume much BBC content at all, but if I do it will be on a TV or smart device.

It provides me and my friends with knowledge and entertainment however, it's not my first option. Netflix is better value – I wish the BBC could be cheaper – if it was more people my age might pay for it.

I do watch BBC news, Peaky Blinders & David Attenborough. The documentaries are pretty good too.

By far the worst thing about the BBC is the licence fee – it's such an old fashioned way of paying.

The service I watch mostly is Netflix, followed by the new Disney streaming service, and also content on YouTube. I get my music from Amazon music because we have a family subscription which means it's free to me. A lot of my friends use Spotify which I would use if I didn't have free access to Amazon.

Chapter 11

To Three or not to Three?
That is the question!

The words 'young people' and the channel 'BBC Three' perhaps gets more mentions than any others in the BBC's annual report for 2020. Political antennas are twitching in Broadcasting House and Auntie is responding. Is this short-term rhetoric or a real strategic pivot? Michael Wilson explores

While audiences in all age groups increased as the Covid-19 lockdown forced many of us to screens of all size to fill our leisure time, the long-term trend for the under-30s is away from the BBC. This is a key issue that concerns Ofcom, the Government (as a policy issue not just a political one) and the BBC itself.

Ofcom did not mince its words in its last annual review of the BBC:

"Like all PSBs, the BBC is vulnerable to the rapidly changing media landscape, particularly in its struggle to attract and retain younger audiences. Unless it can address this, its ability to deliver its Mission and Public Purpose to the same level in the future will be at risk...time spent with the BBC by younger audiences across TV, radio and the BBC's main online site has declined further in 2018/19.

"Our review of the BBC's news and current affairs output also suggests that the BBC is struggling to engage younger audiences with news and current affairs, particularly online. If

the BBC can't engage young audiences with its content, it risks losing a generation of viewers. If young people don't consider the BBC as a core part of their viewing, then it may be hard to encourage them to pay the licence fee which will have significant implications for the BBC's revenue and its ability to deliver its Mission and Public Purpose."

If the BBC doesn't have an audience then the justification for the universal licence fee begins to dramatically weaken. With no licence fee, the scale and scope of the BBC will likely reduce and its ability to service audiences will be challenging. A vicious circle of reducing funding, reducing scale and reducing scope.

The BBC responded in May 2020 in its annual report. Its two-year plan aims to increase engagement with young people and has proposed nine action points including shifting commissioning spend, more boxsets on the iPlayer, investment in BBC Sounds, a 'story-led' approach to news plus a new news app and better tracking and research. The action point that gained the most interest and column inches was this:

"Exploring the options available to BBC Three in developing its profile online and possibly through the restoration of a linear channel."

Is it regulatory overreach?

The BBC has not reacted well to independent regulation – it was only at the last Royal Charter where much regulation moved from the internal BBC Trust to the external Ofcom. The regulator, both publicly and even more vocally privately, is tired of the BBC not being open and accountable in respect to the decisions it makes. This has to change – the public pay for the BBC – an independent regulator has the right to judge transparently its performance and actions.

However how their services are delivered is for the BBC and the BBC alone. For Ofcom to so specifically flag young people is perhaps regulatory over-reach. Many parts of the UK audience, both demographically and geographically are under represented both on and off air.

Ofcom has previously cited 'older women' and 'portrayal' of different regions and communities as being under served by the BBC, but there is far less concern about these group than for the young eyeballs and ears.

The BBC has an Asian network, but not an Afro-Caribbean one. At this time when #BlackLivesMatter has prominence, is this maybe a more relevant gap in audiences being served?

And, interestingly, while Ofcom has a remit for media literacy, surely the BBC should also play a regulated role in addressing media literacy as the major public service media organisation for the whole of the United Kingdom?

Is Three really the magic number?

There are plenty of other issues for Ofcom, so why is the regulator so hung up on this one?

Should the BBC be reallocating significant sums chasing just one part of the whole audience? In an email exchange while researching this book, presenter and business woman Sarah Greene said, it's impossible to call 'young people' one audience.

This is at the core of the BBC's problem with a young audience. It takes huge resource to get volume, it takes even bigger resource to get reach. A number of contributors to this book – especially Marcus Ryder in Chapter 16 and Claire Hungate in Chapter 8 discuss the success of Netflix catering for niches and growing their business model by delivering content to underserved audiences.

Broadcasting on linear television is expensive – you need to have schedulers, engineers, transmission teams, big infrastructure networks, pay for satellite space and DTT spectrum. Many of these costs fall away – or are much smaller – in an on-demand world.

YouTube has a bigger audience, in terms of young people, than the BBC and it is not a TV channel; Netflix pulls large audiences, it is not a TV channel; Disney+ has millions of subscribers and it is not…you get the point. Indeed since beginning to write this chapter Disney has announced it will closer all Disney-branded UK channels. Clearly it has a strategy that's non-linear!

And the BBC also delivers huge results with some online content. There have been close to 40m separate requests to watch the adaptation of Sally Rooney's novel *Normal People*, via the BBC iPlayer, with many binge-watching the series. However it must be pointed out that, even though the BBC claims *Normal People* as a huge hit with young people, 60 per cent of those viewing on the iPlayer were older than 35.

The BBC Three television audience was never huge. It was 22 per cent in 2015/16 when it was a linear television service. Now remember that's 22 per cent of the 16-34 audience, not the total audience.

Since BBC Three was taken off linear television in March 2016 its weekly reach with the 16-34 demographic has levelled off at around at eight per cent over the past two years. But that doesn't mean only eight per cent of this age group consume the BBC – it is of course far higher. By creating niche channels, then the BBC allows the data to be a stick it can be beaten with.

The BBC annual report for 2020 talks about boosting funding for BBC Three by £40m (to around £80m) and then states that cuts have to be made in other channels and genres to accommodate that.

These cuts, plus cost savings of £125m because of losses in commercial trading from BBC Studios due to Covid-19 and having to delay implementation of their over-75 licence pushback, mean many painful headlines about BBC job losses and service reductions will outstrip any wins in the under-30s audience for months to come.

The annual plan praises the strong performance of BBC Three scripted programming including *Fleabag*, *Killing Eve* and *Normal People*. As well as being available on the iPlayer that also have slots on BBC One after the *News at Ten* where top BBC Three shows are scheduled three nights a week. Other successes have included *My Left Nut*, *Killed By My Debt* (which won a Bafta), the Stacey Dooley documentaries and *RuPaul's Drag Race*.

The annual report states:

"Our research evidence shows that there is a big available audience on linear television and the BBC could reach them if we move decisively. So there is potentially a strong case for restoring BBC Three as a linear channel as well as an online destination."

Utter rubbish.

A confused argument

The debate around returning BBC Three to linear television is confused, more aimed perhaps at delivering a regulatory tick, than a new audience. As the young audience moves to on-demand then so should the BBC. The iPlayer will be the entry point for the BBC in the years ahead. Not just for young eyeballs but all viewers – so far in 2020 there has been a 60 per cent plus increase in programme requests via the iPlayer compared to 2019.

The BBC even admits a linear channel would be secondary in audience to online:

"While young people would continue to predominately watch BBC Three content online."

The additionality of a linear channels would be marginal, the costs would be significant at a time when all budgets are under review. Sure, invest in the content, but think radically about the distribution. Plus the success of these BBC Three programmes is *because* they are on the main BBC One service.

BBC Three had an ok electronic programme guide (EPG) position, but was not on page 1 of any EPG. High-quality BBC Three programming can be shown on BBC One. Just like dramas such as *Line of Duty* and comedy like *Have I Got News For You* moved from BBC Two to BBC One.

This happened too when BBC Three launched in 2003 and made its name with hits like *Little Britain* and *Gavin and Stacey*. These programmes transferred to main channels. Indeed the biggest show on television for Christmas 2019 was a *Gavin and Stacey* reboot on BBC One.

That's what good programming and development means – making hits, developing (British) talent and then selling to other international broadcasters to help fund more programming and bring less reliance on the licence fee. BBC Three's commissioning team has been very good at finding 'hits', but it's impossible to translate across a whole channels – both on cost grounds and the shortage of stand-out ideas.

There is no reason why BBC Three online hits cannot move to existing linear channels and grow – BBC Three does not need its own channel.

The reason these hit programmes have shown "there is a big available audience on linear television" is that not just young people are watching. The argument stands – 'hit' programming attracts larges audiences across *all* age groups.

The BBC clearly defines a 'hit' as a programme that get a high volume of audience and/or critical acclaim. But a hit should also be a programme that serves very well a niche audience, may not get a high audience rating, but is also critically successful.

The BBC always says it doesn't chase the ratings – but the truth is a commissioner or channel heads are judged as being good or effective on the volume of audience, not the reach of the service. Look at their channel – and often their personal – social media feeds, it's the big audiences and the awards they celebrate, not the new audiences reached.

How the BBC reacts

The BBC annual report also states:

"We'd be wrong not to back a service that is doing better than anyone could have ever conceived."

This is BBC-speak for we have been told to 'back a service' which is now politically important. The report beautifully contradicts itself too stating, *"Investing in digital services means the BBC is better meeting the demands of audiences, particularly younger people."*

So do young people want 'linear' or 'digital'? Or is the BBC just smattering the words 'young people' in the document as much as it can to show they are on the corporate radar. The shiny new corporate buzz phrase!

The BBC is watched and listened to by the young audiences on BBC One, on BBC Two and BBC Four (with great quality content covering arts, science, foreign drama – often more cutting edge than any other channels), local and national radio, on the apps and on the iPlayer.

For the BBC to belong to everyone and for the young audience to grow with the BBC as they become a family audience, a middle-aged audience and then the older audiences, they need to see and hear the breadth all of the services the BBC delivers.

Young Asians have programming on the BBC Asian Network; young Scots have some fabulous music and comedy programming on BBC Radio Scotland; and when I drive around the country, some of the most passionate new music programming comes from BBC local radio – I could refer you back to *The Beat* on BBC East Midlands mentioned in the Forward to this book.

It is sometimes possible to believe that many at the heart of the BBC machine in Broadcasting House don't see what the tentacles of the organisation do and where the organisation really touches the audience.

Look at the New Voices' project –said to be "the biggest talent search in the history of BBC local radio." In one weekend more than 3,500 people were auditioned. Online trade publication *Radio Today* reports: "420 have already been given opportunities to present, report and contribute on air on stations across the country….and let's have younger voices as part of the mix in the right places."

Every part of the BBC needs to serve in some way every possible part of the audience to be relevant. It's that argument about volume and reach again.

About the writer

Michael Wilson is co-editor of this book.

Sound bite #7

Mark Curry, presenter, Blue Peter ,1986-89; Record Breakers, The Saturday   Picture Show 1982-86

I have always felt slightly disappointed that young people's television was put onto a designated channel because programmes such as Blue Peter, Record Breakers and The Saturday Picture Show were always watched by a family audience, hence a larger cross section of people.

Content in these programmes was of interest to all ages, despite being produced by the children's programme department. I don't know why CBBC was created but I do know it produces some quality programmes for kids and young people.

My two under-30 godsons prefer Netflix, Amazon Prime or YouTube because they seem to them to be a 'cool' watch.

Perhaps this age group will dip into the soaps if they feel they can relate to certain storylines and Love Island is a massive hit. We are living in an age, I think, where there is a great emphasis on the 'new', the 'latest', the 'fast' and that word again, the 'cool'...

Chapter 12

Not just any old channel

The BBC is a radio and television broadcaster like no other. It has a unique position and an inherited responsibility in the culture of civilisation…Wow – but true! Farrukh Dhondy's argument is that it can retain that role by adjusting to contemporary competition and times

It was not quite Covid-19, but some crisis of the 1990s and we, the commissioning editors of Channel 4 at the time, had been called together to discuss it.

One of our number, whom I shall not name, as he has gone on to be a renowned producer of content, in an ill-considered moment, said: "At times like this one turns to the BBC". There was stunned silence round the rectangular table. The supremo, one Michael Grade, said: "What?"

Here we were, the providers, under a parliamentary remit, of themes and programmes that other channels, including the BBC, did not offer. We were there around the rectangular table to consider how we could address, in a characteristically unique way, the immediate challenge of the crisis.

(I solemnly declare that I've forgotten what it was, however important it seemed at the time.)

In the face of severe competition, from the massive expanse of television in the shape of channels offering specific, alluring and competitive content, Channel 4 has joined the prat- race. The 'remit' is now akin to granny's recipes in an age of tempting fast food.

My colleague from those decades past, was correct in his blurted, subconscious conviction that the BBC is not just one of the then existing channels, including its first competitors, the ITV channels in their regional avatars; it was intended as soon as the technology became available, as the social conversation of the nation.

It could pretend, in addition to being the party to which all were invited, to take on the role of the ecclesiastical gathering and arrogantly assume to be the impartial, sometimes preachy, conscience of the nation.

The aims have changed

Yes, yes, yes, I know – the pompous and brilliant Lord Reith said 'inform, educate, entertain' and no other first lord of the BBC has admitted to adding to these ambitions or to very deliberately pushing these guiding stars around the welkin or even to slyly reinterpreting them.

And even without any acknowledged or avowed alteration of these aims we now have Auntie dedicated, in combatting the competition, to *prurience, plebeian popularity* and *politically-correct pretension*.

Survival is all. In the competitive field of TV and the proliferation of web platforms, the BBC has no choice but to embrace and expand in all three of these fields and, while not abandoning its role as the central conversation of the nation, reconsider how to turn these three Ps into dignified contributions to the information, education and entertainment of the nation.

Consider, gentle reader, what the BBC has been and should be. It arose from the liberal conscience of one of the advanced nations of the world. Advanced, not only in its rule over the most extensive empire history has known, but with a tradition of liberal thought that went beyond the lies and manipulation of vested, political or religiously bigoted interests, to enlist the ethics of balance, truth and human decency and progress.

It was conceived as free of the bias of support for one political faction or another; it embraced objectivity in its reporting and attempted to be the cultural arbiter of the nation. It was not owned, as the TV channels that have proliferated after it and have become a tsunamic presence today, by profit-makers or those with an ideological bias or some dictatorial national partisanship.

As such, its international operations acquired a reputation for fair presentation that no other enterprise, owned in the US, Middle East, Russia or China, enjoyed. But this untainted international reputation is not going to be part of any consideration of its future – its competitors and their political spokespersons and media puppets will see to that.

The BBC, as an institution cannot and must not occupy the same status as any other broadcasting entity. Around the world, these exist for three purposes – to be the voice of the government, to preach some religious or cultist doctrine and to make a profit for owners or shareholders. The BBC was founded for none of these and, though it may have occasionally appeared to have been defiled by one or other of these *raisons d'etre,* it remains, or retains as its ideal, what it should be: Britain's contribution to the conversation of civilisation.

Civilisation takes inconvenient or awkward turns. Young viewers, the generations between teenage and the 30s, are, according to statistics, turning to the sex-and-violence-filled menu of the dramas and shows of the web series or to the substitute prurience of programmes such as *Love Island.* Must the BBC compete?

The answer has to be 'yes' if it is to maintain the attention of this generation, but that can't be an imitative 'yes' without distorting, out of recognition, Auntie's character.

The dramatisation of violence and sex are globally inherited human traditions and international epics from *The Iliad* to *The Mahabharata*, and the more thoughtful canon of novels and plays, have bestowed on us an inheritance of linking their portrayal or appearance to a moral or social purpose.

In a contemporary rendition, *Romeo and Juliet* or *Antony and Cleopatra* can, and no doubt will, be pictured making unfettered (sic) love. But will that be a gratuitous addition or a portrayal of the experience which Shakespeare didn't dare to elaborate?

And so, with the opposite portrayal of violence-in-sex, as in the multiple and gang-rapes of the central character Phoolan Devi in a film I commissioned for Channel 4 called *Bandit Queen*. It was a statement against the violence and power-balance of the Indian caste system and traditional injustice and cruelty of the gender equation. Those who perceived the depiction in the film as prurient must have had very sad sex lives.

That being said, producers, directors and writers for the BBC, though conscious that Jane Austen didn't write sex scenes into her novels, have spiced up their adaptations with lots of it. It does nothing additional for the BBC's pride or its prejudices, except that it seems to have swallowed the first having acquired the other, in the form of a conviction that it brings in non-literary audiences. Does it?

There are, even on the BBC, drama series with sex scenes and there need be no squeamishness about these if they serve an emotional, moral or social purpose in the drama – espousing the rights of women, even exposing the deviant sexual prejudices or oppressions of certain communities. Which is not to say that drama can't incorporate the joys of the process of consensual seduction with stimulating explicitness. Perhaps that was what D'Arcy was doing with Elizabeth?

Channel 4's remit

From its inception and perhaps through two decades, certainly through the period from 1984 to 1997, when I served as one of its commissioning editors, Channel 4 was consciously dedicated to the execution of its remit.

The paradox of the remit was that, being enjoined to do what other channels did not, we had to find, not the most outlandish invented formats and territories to explore, but those which were under the nation's very noses and had received no attention. So, on the Channel, the tide of feminist assertion gave rise to programmes in all genres and the issues of gay existence – not simply the assertion of gay rights – were firmly. in focus.

In my own area of multi-cultural programming, it meant putting to one side, rather than completely ignoring, the prevalent, liberality-assuaging mission-to-complain – and getting down instead to explore, through every possible televisual genre, the life, issues and ebullience of the new communities of Britain.

To join the national conversation, this couldn't be an exercise in positive images or providing role models! That should be left to Saatchi and Saatchi and other advertising agencies who sell the positive images of brands of toothpaste or detergent. As a prescription for the portrayal or presence of ethnic people on television, it would be demeaning and an insult to treat us as needing such a sales pitch.

If the drama, the investigations, the chat shows, the films, the observational documentaries, the news reports, the arts programmes, the situation comedies had to engage, entertain or convince the general population, they had to have a warts-and-all remit.

It worked, in tandem with reports of black and Asian contributory activities and triumphs, through documentary series, through programmes such as *The Bandung File*, *Black*

Bag, *Devil's Advocate*, *Quarrels*, the situation comedies such as *Desmond's* and a hundred more.

The age (or scourge?) of diversity then invaded the channel and inevitably the BBC. Yes, we are all happy to see black actors playing protagonists' parts in Shakespeare and other prestigious drama – and it makes a community proud and asserts the virtue of directors and the industry. But it doesn't integrate the isolated, ignored communities into the discourse of the nation.

Why, for instance, was there never an inkling through investigation, observation or even in drama, any hint, of what was going on in Rochdale, Rotherham, Oxford and the communities in which predominantly Muslim gangs were grooming vulnerable girls? Why did no investigative crew penetrate the presence and network of persuasion that made 15-year-old Bangladeshi girls run off to Syria to join Isis?

What profit-seeking channels cannot do

The profit-seeking channels will not and probably cannot fulfil such a function. The BBC can and should turn its attention to including in its liberal-minded 'diversity' not only a black actor's face as Coriolanus and the appointment behind the camera of competent BAME-wallas, but bringing the skills of the media to present and debate the veiled, the hidden and the unseen.

Fifty ways of doing this, fulfilling this prescription, come instantly to mind – but it's not the purpose of this piece to pitch or to do the BBC's job for it! BBC Three, now a web-channel, should be financed as the ideal vehicle to challenge youth-oriented competitors such as Vice, which relies on access to programmes through phones and devices not localised in front rooms. The right strategy would be to adequately finance it to compete, even with Netflix and Amazon.

In considering the programming possibilities within the dimension of plebeian popularity, an essay by Orwell comes to mind in which, considering the British character, he makes a list.

Apart from his initial assertions that the British are averse to being called intellectual and are, justifiably, called hypocritical and double-faced, he notices the universal British love of flowers. He goes on to say: "We are also a nation of stamp-collectors, pigeon-fanciers, amateur carpenters, coupon-snippers, dart-players, crossword-puzzle fans."

The attention that only a nationally-conscious channel such as the BBC can and must give to these characteristics or plebeian pastimes is manifest in the popularity of shows such as *Gardeners' Question Time*, the *Bake-off* competitions, the *Antique Road Show* and darts and word-quizzes – which in many instances garner more viewers and listeners than the sex and violence shows of the web. Orwell's list certainly needs up-dating but exploring this vein leads to the heart of what Auntie can do for and with contemporary enthusiasms.

The BBC is threatened, not only by competition but by unimaginative political interference, with the unseen hand of vested interests posing as political anti-licence-fee determinants.

Just as we find the NHS necessary and pay for it through taxes, so should it be with the BBC. Yes, there certainly is a strong argument for demolishing, and not simply reforming, the Kafkaesque structures of its decision-making, which are not only wasteful but editorially compromising and the enemy of diverse (not 'Diverse') and imaginative innovation with a handful of overlords taking the final decisions. New wardrobes, face lifts, and possibly a strict diet for Auntie as the medicine – and an end to this talk of capital punishment.

About the writer

Farrukh Dhondy is an Indo-British writer of fiction, non-fiction, TV, stage and film. He was commissioning editor for multicultural programmes at Channel 4 between 1984 and 1997.

Chapter 13

A TikToking clock heading towards regeneration – or not?

How do young people consume content? Does the manner in which they do provide any clues to how they might engage with the BBC in the future? Colin Mann finds out first hand from a group of teenagers on their thoughts on the corporation and whether these insights offer any hope. It might be an uphill struggle

In seeking to address the issues raised in this book, I found myself at an early disadvantage: no close family who could be categorised as the 'missing generation', and under lockdown, no easy prospect of gauging their thoughts on the matter.

However, a close associate with children falling into that demographic, and whose kids' school and college friends were keen to contribute, undertook to host an online discussion.

At the outset, one participant admitted that they hadn't watched the BBC since actor Matt Smith "stopped being *Doctor Who*", around 2014, when he was replaced by the older Peter Capaldi.

This group, although far from what might be considered an empirical sample, proved very opinionated and passionate about the topic, particularly in terms of their current perception of the corporation and its funding model.

"The BBC is irrelevant to our generation," declared one. "You don't get taxed for watching things online," added another. All participants saw the licence fee as a tax, with the potential penalties for non-payment a cause for concern. "If you don't pay, you go to jail," observed one. "It's like *1984*."

"The more they try to force us to pay, the less we want to watch," waned another.

What one participant described as 'bundling' was not favoured. "I only want to watch *Killing Eve*, not the rest. Why should I pay if I don't want to watch all of it?"

"Forcing people to pay is where it's going wrong," said another, with others agreeing that they would be happy to pay to watch it on another platform.

"The BBC should concentrate on making programmes and sell to the Netflixes," was one suggestion. "You can engage with that platform and will pay for that content."

"We know the BBC has got to make money somehow, we know that's how it is, but we just don't agree with how they are doing it," summed up one contributor. There certainly wasn't a sense that this group wanted 'something for nothing'.

A question of image

The perception of the licence fee as a 'tax' will prove problematic for the BBC as it seeks to ensure that this generation, who will become wage-earners in the coming years, continue to contribute to the corporation's finances. They all expressed their willingness to pay for the content they like and professed to eschew piracy.

The group was clear as to how it saw the BBC. "What I hate most, is that it's old-fashioned, mumsy and patronising," admitted one contributor. "Yes, it's fuddy-duddy," agreed another. One source of annoyance were programme interstitials, with the suggestion that this was just 'propaganda'. "I have no patience for it."

Indicating perhaps that there is a misconception as to the BBC's status, one participant ventured that "the BBC is run by the government and I don't trust the Government, so I definitely don't trust the BBC. They are not independent and they spew out propaganda," with another saying: "They certainly don't represent people like us". Another felt the BBC was "too political".

"We don't feel we're getting the whole story from the BBC; it only panders to small section and everyone else feels disenfranchised," was one observation. "It's non-inclusive, it's left-wing, London-centric and not an organisation for young people," was one accusation .

"They are like the Civil Service," suggested one. "Their content is rubbish; they make it for themselves, not for us," ventured another, who added: "They need to function like a business, and sell us what we want".

For some participants, it was not necessarily the BBC's content that was the problem, but the platform itself. "I'll watch BBC content on Netflix, because it is legal," admitted one. The multiplicity of SVOD options is also problematic. "All these different platforms are a pain; we just want one or two for everything," complained one.

Back in November 2018, Sharon White, then Ofcom CEO, called for UK public service broadcasters (PSBs) to form a combined catch-up platform in order to be more like Netflix. On-demand provider BritBox was launched in the UK in 2019 but the PSBs still have their own catch-up platforms. And since then Disney+ has joined Netflix and Prime Video in the SVOD marketplace, further complicating the ease of access issue.

In describing what content this sample consumes, and how, Netflix, Amazon, YouTube, TikTok and Starz were mentioned as popular platforms, and apps.

"I like to binge a series, not waste a whole week," admitted one. "There's a lot of [BBC] content that's not relevant. YouTube gives each person what they want to see and there's far more of it."

Of those who were familiar with the UK PSB online services, ITV Hub was not favoured. "There are too many ads, it's hard to navigate and there is too much junk," was a typical gripe, which suggests that any form of ad-supported BBC platform is not in favour. The group was not impressed by ads overall, with a number admitting to using ad-blockers.

Suggesting that the BBC operates a 'long-tail' model, one contributor said that the BBC tends "only to go where there's a big audience", with the group agreeing that they want "very niche content".

Although there is an indication that this generation is willing to pay for BBC content, a hybrid, AVOD (advertisement based video on demand) would not appear to be an option.

Those favouring YouTube found people on the platform "very knowledgeable", saying that you can engage and talk with the people who made the video and they will talk back. Authenticity and engagement were important, with users often going to the 'Comments' section first to discover their peers' thoughts.

In terms of sharing views on content, it is worth noting that the discussion took place just before the BBC launched its *BBC Together* initiative, designed to enable family, friends, and classmates to watch and listen to BBC programmes together even when they are apart, enabling people to watch and listen to video and audio content from iPlayer, Sounds, Bitesize, news and sport at exactly the same time.

A later follow-up with a smaller section of the group ascertained that, novel though the idea was, it didn't really chime with their viewing habits and social interactions.

"We go to TikTok and YouTube because we can say what we think. It's not curated. The BBC is like it's run by teachers; TikTok and YouTube are more like the playground. You can chat with your friends, it's real, it's now, it's relevant," was the verdict.

"No-one I know watches the BBC, it's not what we talk about. We talk about what's on Netflix," one revealed. "When Netflix releases a big show, we're all talking about it and Instagramming," another added.

And the future?

The idea of communal, shared viewing was a somewhat alien concept, with few admitting to watching linear TV with friends and family. "I watch on my own although sometimes I do watch movies with others," was the closest admission.

As to availability and relevance of content, the market-leading SVODs were favoured. "There's loads to watch on Amazon and Netflix. The recommendations on [those platforms] work really well," was one testimonial.

Although expressing a willingness to pay for content, the omens do not look good for BritBox. "Why should they charge for things made years ago?"

It is apparent that this group don't watch content with other people, they watch it on their own, but they want to share it and talk about it afterwards. The idea of sitting down and watching something on TVs went out about ten years ago; they are watching on mobile devices.

"They have no future in their current form," contended one. "It's not too late for them to change, but they need to do things they are not willing to do. They are too blinkered and too deaf."

Summarising the discussion, it was clear that the group had no confidence that the BBC understands their generation or was willing to change; and even if it were willing to change, that would not be enough to make them want to pay the licence fee.

What emerged was that if the BBC called it a subscription, and said it would cost £12 a month to subscribe to this content service, the group would see it completely differently. It was a choice to subscribe, not an enforced action.

There is a misunderstanding that their generation is pirating; they don't need to do that anymore. There is so much content available that they can view legally.

This generation are also content creators. Platforms such as YouTube, TikTok and Instagram take up a lot of their time. They are interacting and creating content of their own.

Initiatives such as *BBC Together* may go some way to re-engaging this generation, but the problem of content relevance still remains an issue.

In closing, one parent and offspring who contributed to the discussion agreed with the earlier observation regarding Peter Capaldi replacing Matt Smith as *Doctor Who*, led to their break from linear TV, suggesting the move typified the decreasing relevance of the BBC. A regeneration too far perhaps? The corporation's 'Doctors' have regenerated; the question now is: "Can the BBC?"

About the writer

Colin Mann has more than 40 years' experience in the media and communications industries. His early career was with BT in a range of commercial and regulatory roles, in particular with the cable and satellite TV unit, long before the telco became a broadcaster in its own right.

Operating as an independent consultant since 1990, his clients have included satellite TV channels, telcos and cable TV operators. He has edited *Euromedia* magazine since 2000 and is an associate editor of advanced-television.com. He also acts as media analyst for specialist consultancy Omnisperience.

Colin is a Fellow of the Society of Broadband Professionals (SCTE) and a member of both the Royal Television Society and Broadcasting Press Guild. He can be contacted on colinmann@cix co.uk; Twittter@colincmann

Sound bite #8

Peter Purves, presenter, *Blue Peter* 1967-78

I have to confess to having lost a lot of my faith in the BBC's impartiality over the past few years and, as a consequence, watch very little of its news coverage. I feel it is too full of the reporters' own views, opinions and analysis, rather than the reporting of facts.

There is still much to admire that the BBC does well. Its new drama is often very good, but to use the old cliché, it has dumbed down to quite a low level, particularly in its lack of imagination in programming. I think it is laughable to follow a cooking show with a cooking show with a repeated antique programme following a repeated Escape to wherever. Boring and uninspiring.

So it does not surprise me that the younger generation has moved away from the Beeb, and finds its pleasure in other platforms. It is only to be expected that there is a limit as to how much good quality TV there is. When there were three or four channels, then there seemed to be a never-ending delight of top-notch programmes.

With the proliferation of other channels and platforms, there is still the same amount of quality programmes, but they are harder to find and spread widely across the board. With these different channels the corporation has gone out to chase the audience but has spread itself too thin in every way.

Chapter 14

One channel, too many competing interests?

In 2019, the BBC established a designated digital Scotland channel to address the complex challenges of giving more space to Scottish-made programmes. Maurice Smith asks if the initial result is that youth needs have been neglected and whether more must be done to please its Scottish audience, both young and old

The BBC is in a state of flux. Close watchers might observe that the corporation is often in such a state. Any organisation which depends on a charter that requires it to spend every few years lobbying for its very *raison d'etre* is likely to suffer the same neurosis.

Right now, in the wake of the Conservatives' overwhelming 2019 election victory, and with significant political change such as Brexit in train, the strategists at W1A would always have existed in a heightened state of uncertainty as they grapple with the future.

Politicians (in the form of the then-Chancellor Gordon Brown in 1999) left a hand-grenade in the laundry when they decided that all households containing an over-75-year-old would be entitled to a free licence fee. When one of Brown's successors, George Osborne, forced the BBC in 2015 to take on the Treasury's responsibility for this massive and growing subsidy, the organisation weakly accepted a burden it could not afford.

Now it is being bullied in the court of public opinion as the meanie penalising well-off pensioners – the poor, remember, won't be paying a license fee in any case – by charging them for TV and radio consumption.

The Johnson administration seems happy to revel in the BBC's discomfiture. Dominic Cummings, the Rasputin of Downing Street, seems to view the broadcaster as a bastion of liberalism and therefore a target.

He threatens the de-criminalisation of licence-fee evasion, and even an earlier-than-usual review of the next Royal Charter, to destabilise the BBC further.

Why not replace the fee with a subscription service? Why not open everything to the free market? The truth is if politicians did not have the BBC to threaten, cajole and generally kick around, they would have to invent a new version. And a BBC that became reliant on subscriptions or advertising income might quickly become a commercial threat to other media players.

Plenty of issues in Scotland and elsewhere

The BBC has other issues too. There is the question of on-screen representation of minorities, a concern that has gained momentum thanks to an initiative led originally by the comedian Lenny Henry and amplified more recently by the Black Lives Matter (BLM) campaign. There is the competition from new services such as Netflix and Amazon. And there is the challenge presented by falling interest among the young in conventional broadcasting.

In Scotland, there is an added collection of issues to add to a virtual Venn diagram of disquiet facing the BBC. It is articulated generally within the ongoing constitutional debate about Scotland's relationship with the rest of the United Kingdom, for which the BBC has become an awkward cypher.

For 30 years, the BBC has known from its own research that it super-serves white middle-class and middle-aged people – especially men – in London and the south-east of England. Imagine a graph that follows a map of contentment with BBC services; as it moves north and north-west towards Scotland and Northern Ireland, levels of satisfaction – and licence-fee payment compliance, not uncoincidentally – fall steadily. Devolution in 1999 and the Good Friday Agreement might have ameliorated the general situation, but in truth the BBC was slow to respond to their impact and found itself caught in the spotlight of political discord at key points including the 2014 Scottish independence referendum.

In February 2019, the BBC launched BBC Scotland, a new digital channel intended to give more space to Scottish-made programmes. The channel has been envisaged by the BBC as a means of answering criticism on several fronts, and to provide a platform for locally-made news and factual programmes, as well as some entertainment and arts programming.

The channel exists to some extent as a response to the oft-repeated criticism that the BBC spends considerably less on programmes originated in Scotland than it collects in licence fee income. By some calculations the gap is around £100m. In Scotland, where so much public discourse is coloured by the sense that 'London' deals the country an unfair hand, that matters a great deal.

In 2017, when the BBC first proposed a channel, the move was a clear response to the spending issue – which had identified as an issue by the BBC Trust – and also to the fact that Scots had emerged as those least convinced of the corporation's relevance in the multi-channel, digital age.

A year earlier, the Scottish advisory committee of the regulator Ofcom quoted the BBC's own research as follows: "There is a persistent measurable public purpose gap, with research from the BBC showing that only 48 per cent of Scots think the BBC is good at representing their life in news and current affairs content, the lowest in the UK. The BBC continues to fail to adequately reflect and represent Scots both to themselves and to the rest of the UK."

So here was the BBC – under attack generally from more agile competitors which are able to peel off layers of the audience, and habitually from politicians driven by their own biases, whether they be pro or anti-EU or Scottish independence – now attempting to respond to the heartfelt criticism of a Scottish audience.

Was the new channel the answer?

The new channel was presented as an answer to all this. To many within the corporation, it was actually an answer to the earlier vociferous campaign for a 'Scottish Six', an hour of national, international and Scottish news that would have replaced the regional-styled *Reporting Scotland* programme more along the lines of the nightly *Six One* programme of the Irish public broadcaster RTE.

The 'Scottish Six' has been headed off by the BBC hierarchy many times since it was first mooted with the arrival of devolution in the late 1990s. In fact, outgoing director-general Tony Hall – who was to approve the new channel in 2017 – was at the head of BBC News when it fought off Scottish demands for its own 'national' news in 1999. At the time his boss John Birt is alleged to have claimed ominously to the Blair government that such a move might "break up the BBC".

Twenty years later, the Scottish channel has an hour of news, but at 9pm nightly rather than 6pm. Its slot puts it up against major TV drama and documentaries on competing channels. Critics say it has been "designed to fail", although the BBC may argue that the new channel transmits only from 7pm in any case.

The channel's remit also calls for commissioners to find new ways to reach the elusive youth market.

The BBC generally is depending more on the ever-expanding BBC iPlayer to reach viewers under 30, and particularly the 16-25 age group, while the Scottish channel's launch has been augmented by a greater effort online.

Commissioned programmes include those that do not conform to conventional linear durations and also edited versions produced specifically for the web. Young people want their media in digestible bites, and often view content only on a mobile device, and that has forced all broadcasters to adapt their output.

Are Scottish young people any different from those in the rest of the UK? Certainly, compared to other age groups they are the most likely to support independence. But, in terms of media consumption, is that reflected in their tastes?

Anecdotally, no. Scottish twenty-somethings are watching Netflix (very often free, as they catch a spare log-in belonging to friends or family) and YouTube. They are unlikely to watch BBC iPlayer, unless they have free access, and rarely watch conventional TV.

A quick check within my own circle confirmed young people's interest. They will watch YouTube videos that may be political, issues-driven material; for example the Black Lives Matter protests in the US or ongoing coverage of football.

The Scottish humourist Limmy performs for hours almost daily, sometimes being watched by thousands as he plays computer games live. There are online sketches by comedians like Ashley Storrie, memes with a Scottish political theme, numerous websites and social media comments about football.

Are today's young really any less enamoured of the BBC than their parents? Those of us who are way beyond our 20s will remember spending a great deal of time browsing titles in video stores during the 1980s and 1990s, seeking out movies to watch at home. Pre social media and YouTube we had music and sports fanzines and plenty of other alternatives. The difference was that without the smart-phone, our access to media was less freely available, and usually cost money. Young people begrudge paying a licence fee; they probably spend the same amount monthly maintaining a broadband connection.

Taking the strain on many fronts

So, in Scotland, that new digital channel is being asked to take the strain on many fronts: to convince a sceptical audience of the corporation's commitment north of the border, to embrace the digital age, and also to appeal to 'under-served' groups including minorities and the young.

To achieve all this, the annual budget was stated at £31m, although there has been no real public breakdown. Given that the nightly hour of news involved the recruitment of 80 staff and probably costs around £8-9m, that leaves approximately £22m, half of which was spent already on programmes made as opt-outs to BBC Two, a service sacrificed as a price for the channel.

In net terms, the new money for the channel may be not have been much more than £10m, a fraction of the perceived gap between income from Scotland and cash spent there by a corporation whose overall income is more than £3.5bn. And in March 2020, as the channel began its second year of transmission and the UK entered Covid-19 lockdown, that budget is understood to have been reduced.

So the BBC Scotland channel is expected to perform a great deal of heavy lifting, addressing so many issues – political, economic, audience perception – virtually simultaneously.

Incoming director-general Tim Davie and the new BBC Scottish director, who is still to be appointed at the time of writing, will experience a renewed burden of expectation if the SNP achieves a majority and extends its period in power into a fourth successive term in the Scottish parliamentary election due in May 2021.

The pursuit of the youth audience is possibly the least tangible target too. BBC Three – taken off conventional services and placed online-only back in 2016 – is targeted unashamedly at that niche. Its commissioning of programmes embraces non-linear durations and has involved some risk-taking in terms of content. The channel covers issues like sex and drugs in a less conventional fashion, at times resembling rivals such as Vice. But by 2020 it was deemed a success and enjoyed a substantial budget increase.

The BBC Three experience underlines the commercial fact that it is easier to concentrate on a single audience segment – in this case, young viewers – at the expense of others. The same is true of specialist channels covering sports, or the arts, or movies.

But the Scottish channel is being expected to meet many, if not competing then certainly incongruous, interests.

Football programmes appealing to young working class men do not necessarily appeal to an even younger female audience that seeks educational drama or films that reflect their own experiences. Social history is not the same as hard political news, or a late-night experimental arts project.

The channel has been met to some extent by a hostile press. Right-wing papers prefer to portray the whole idea as some kind of sop to nationalism. The left and pro-independence lobby remain convinced that the BBC is irredeemably embedded within the unionist establishment. The rhetoric of 2014 continues to resound everywhere in Scottish public life, and is likely to be revived if there is a second referendum.

Many of the issues that led to the creation of the channel are likely to re-appear on the Scottish agenda when the pandemic is over, and if politics and public life return to 'normal'. The BBC's gesture of 2019 may have to be built upon if it is to improve its standing in the eyes of its Scottish audience.

About the writer

Maurice Smith is a journalist and broadcaster, based in Glasgow. He runs an award-winning independent TV production company, and worked for many years in newspapers and broadcast news.

Chapter 15

Family Guy, me, and those missing viewers

Distinctive services not provided elsewhere are the keys to the BBC's future, says Tim Hartley. If they are not delivered the old question of what the corporation is for will never go away

I was devastated when they said they were going to close BBC Three on Freeview. Never mind news and current affairs or the *Today* programme, Three was the BBC service I most watched; for two reasons – *Family Guy* and *American Dad*. Within weeks though both programmes were snapped up by ITV2 and were back on Freeview. Phew.

You see I was guffawing with Peter Griffin and Stewie in my 50s. Not exactly Three's target audience. And linear BBC Three, like Radio 2's offer of middle-of-the-road music and chat, was giving us programmes which could and were being provided by the market. Nice to have, but not exactly core public service broadcasting.

This is not an attack on the BBC or the licence fee. Until I gained parole after almost 20 years' service, I was a BBC lifer and still believe in public service broadcasting. But is it realistic for the Beeb to continue to serve every single person in Britain almost every day as Tony Hall seems to think it does? And why single out the 'missing generation' for special treatment? For you could argue that with Radios 1 and 6 Music, BBC Three, online, Sounds and all the rest this segment of the audience is pretty well served by the BBC already.

Ofcom doesn't agree and in its 2018/19 annual report it called on the corporation to do more for younger and diverse audiences.

So let's look at what the BBC is proposing for those audiences as set out in *Bringing us closer* its annual plan for 2020-2021.

There is justifiable praise for the way BBC Three has provided a platform for experimentation and 'new, young adult content.' *Fleabag, Normal People* and Stacey Dooley's investigations are all welcome additions to the televisual menu. There is also a hint in the plan that Three may return as a linear channel though 'the key demographic which will continue to watch online.'

It seems the BBC isn't quite sure where this audience lies – online or on the box – and is hedging its bets by backing both. Media consumption is not a binary choice and it's an awkward fact that young people do actually watch traditional television.

Too top down?

The plan's suggestion that the BBC move towards being a curator of content for and by younger people online is a welcome step. BBC Sounds is to be opened up for non-BBC podcasts helping audiences discover 'the best and most relevant content'. But what does the BBC consider the best and most relevant? Who will decide? (It was the then controller of Radio Three who said with a smile some years ago that a partnership was something the BBC 'do' to you.)

As always news is given proper consideration in the annual plan. For too long young news audiences have been talked down to. There's to be a new, personalised version of the news online app and a 'generational shift to a story-led' approach. Sound advice to all journalists I would have thought. This is all good stuff but however welcome they are, these changes sound a bit top down.

There are different ways of ensuring creativity and a little goes a long way when spent on the ground floor. Jeremy Hunt's promotion of local TV stations depended on taking tiny amounts of licence fee money to prop up channels in places like Cardiff, Leeds and Birmingham.

They offered a different, often quirky take on all things local. When the subsidy disappeared so did many of the stations. Wouldn't some of the money spent on Sounds, the online news app and the plethora of BBC services now available have a bigger, more creative impact if it were competitively bid for by people already doing this?

Ofcom also asked the BBC to set out how it intends to improve representation and portrayal.

The BBC's response talks about increasing the number of people from BAME backgrounds in senior positions as well as on-screen. The wider issue of representation and portrayal has huge resonance in my nation, Wales. How often do we hear young Welsh accents on the network?

According to Ofcom's Media Nations report of 2019 viewing among 16-24 year olds in Wales has declined by 61 per cent since 2010 – a steeper decline than the UK average of 49 per cent for this age group. Half the BBC's spend is outside the M25. The move to Salford has given news and sport a more diverse look and sound. Yes, we have Huw Edwards at ten o'clock every night, but in terms of portrayal, apart from *Gavin and Stacey* and a couple of characters in *The Archers*, I am struggling to hear a Welsh voice.

BBC Wales has tried to marry these two problematic issues – programming which represents Wales and which also appeals to a younger audience. It says it spends a sizeable amount of its budget on youth audiences. The coming of age story *In My Skin* and the documentary *Young, Welsh and Pretty Minted* are distinctly Welsh and were co-commissions with BBC Three. Both did more business online than on linear television. BBC

Wales has also commissioned a series of podcasts and launched BBC Sesh where producers work with young talent allowing them to find their voice, particularly in the field of comedy.

The lessons of S4C

The Welsh language broadcaster, S4C, which is also funded by the licence fee, too is grappling with the dual problems of dwindling audiences and how to connect with younger people.

In 2017 it launched *Hansh*, a social-first service offering daily content for audiences aged between 16 and 34. *Hansh* was delivered initially on Facebook, YouTube and as a weekly TV highlights package. It has expanded onto Twitter, Instagram and TikTok and now offers podcasts and documentaries.

There is a spin-off news and current affairs service called *Hansh Dim Sbin* which provides a space for trainee journalists to create content and develop their skills. It has a different agenda and tone and tackles issues like politics, the Covid-19 pandemic, LGBT+, mental health, climate change, refugees, homelessness and charity work overseas.

Hansh initially incorporated music content aimed at younger audiences, but this was spun off under the new brand *Lŵp*. In 2019 S4C aired the online-first drama series *Merched Parchus* (Respectable Girls) aimed at the 16-34 audience. *Hansh* now has over 50,000 followers across social platforms. Viewing and engagement have grown to a peak of 1.5m views across all platforms. Around 70 per cent of the audience is in the target demographic.

Like the BBC, S4C believes it must reach out to the younger audience if it is to survive in a multi-channel/multi-device world. Visibility is even harder to achieve for smaller broadcasters. The aim of *Hansh* is to build the audience where they go and establish brand trust so that when they do search for longer form content they are guided to it. Social and online-first content is increasingly funded out of the broader content commissioning budget and there has been a gradual shift towards social and digital.

It's a fine balance between giving your main audience what they want and going the whole hog on digital and alternative platforms. S4C generates a huge amount of content in order to fill a traditional linear schedule. Its core Welsh-speaking audience is disproportionately old. Would it benefit from spending more online to try to attract younger viewers and users? Would doing less on TV offer a better return on investment? That is the direction they seem to be heading to.

Is content really king?

But why does any of this matter? Haven't we been told time and again that content is king? Audiences watch good programmes from wherever they come. Netflix and Sky don't define programmes by audience demographics, they don't have a 16-35 section. They don't care. They allow the audience to decide what they want to watch and simply place content in genres to aid searchability.

With Netflix, Amazon Prime, Disney, You Tube, Instagram and the rest just the stroke of a finger away, the question then is what price do we put on distinctively British (or indeed Welsh) creativity?

In terms of volume much of our media is rooted in a wholly American experience. I suspect this is even more the case for young people.

The cultural consequences of globalisation could be no local or national references or shared knowledge. Some would say it doesn't matter, let the market decide. I have a suspicion that whatever the political posturing on the licence fee as an 'unnecessary tax', at a time of constitutional uncertainty, the Beeb will continue to be seen as one of the few enduring, loved and wholly British institutions.

There is a danger that in a post-Covid world, television advertising will continue to collapse. If Channel 4 and ITV were to dilute their public service commitments, the central cultural role of the BBC would become even more important.

It's difficult to argue against the need for a shared place to go for live TV, major events, big sporting occasions and, as we have recently seen, for independent news and comment in times of crisis. You simply cannot summon up this common public space as the need arises.

As a young manager during the Birt regime I remember poring over the 'Hundred Tribes' analysis. The BBC had commissioned this ground-breaking segmentation of the TV market. It came in a glossy tome with graphs and diagrams describing the aspirations of very different groups of people by class, interest, occupation and of course, age. I loved it. But were we really going to serve 100 different tribes?

Let's not be too quick to beat ourselves up about all this. The BBC is still 24 per cent of all UK video, audio and online time spent by adults. Netflix? Just three per cent. The corporation has guaranteed funding offering a certainty which commercial operators would kill for. However, if the BBCs finances are squeezed even more so in these post-Covid times, it cannot be business as usual.

As the new Director-General, Tim Davie, gets his feet under the table there will have to be prioritisation. If he cannot offer distinctive services not provided elsewhere, including properly serving the nations and regions, then the question, "what is the BBC for?" will again be asked. In terms of reinvention and of future proofing perhaps this drive for more, and more creative provision for the 'missing generation', may not be a bad place to start.

About the writer

Tim Hartley is a journalist and author. He has worked for the BBC as a reporter and editor, was Head of News at the Welsh Government and Director of Corporate Affairs at S4C. He was chair of the Royal Television Society in Wales, is a non-executive director of the Co-operative Press and the Welsh Football Trust and is a magistrate sitting on the Cardiff bench. His first volume of travel writing, *Kicking off in North Korea,* was published in 2016. If you can't get him on the phone he'll probably be on top of a mountain riding his bike or watching his beloved Cardiff City. Follow Tim on twitter @timhhartley

Vox Populi

Tau Qureshi, 23, student, Darlington

I get my BBC content mainly online as its easier to navigate through the amount of content they have. The BBC sports app and the iPlayer app are better than their webpages.

Me and my friends use the information and news shown on the BBC sites and use it as comparison to other news we have heard or seen.

I do wish the BBC would keep old and new content on the iPlayer for a much longer period and its services need far better personalisation to give me more control of the channels and categories I see.

The BBC also has to stop creating click-bait stories and gaslighting.

Chapter 16

Welcome to our world, BBC... perhaps

As 2020 began, Neil Fowler believed the nation's licence-funded broadcaster, under pressure from the new government to justify its role, was making the same mistakes that the regional and local press made in the early 2000s. The current health crisis may have helped it find an escape route, but then again...

It's not quite a lifetime ago though, as I write towards the end of the lockdown caused by the Covid-19 pandemic, it certainly seems like it. But it was back in November 2011 that I concluded my year at Nuffield College in Oxford after looking at the decline and future of the regional and local press in the UK with some gloomy predictions.

And, while the sector has changed in a number of ways, its fundamental issue of a spiralling decline in income has not been overcome.

The problems facing the sector (and to all others in the world of printed general news, too) had been pretty clear since the early 2000s as the burgeoning Internet both gave a new and accessible source of news and began the steady decline in advertising yields.

That the whole industry, nationals included, then made the suicidal decision to give away its valuable content for free only gave the anticipated decline a massive downward shove – a judgement from which the industry in general, despite some major rethinks and some hefty investments in paid-for models, has not really recovered.

The regional sector reached a financial summit in about 2003. Margins were enormous after 20 years of continuous growth; there had been massive spends on technology and colour presses; staffing levels had increased dramatically; shareholders were happy; senior executives and analysts seemed to believe all was well and that the good life was here to stay. It might be fair to say there was a whiff of arrogance about the place.

As 2020 arrived I wondered if the BBC, as it struggled to deliver a coherent future strategy against a growing feeling that it had to change dramatically, might be ignoring some of the same broad questions the regional and local sector had so successfully scorned.

Nearly 15 years ago print faced (and continues to face) the perfect storm described above. The BBC in 2020 now has its own perfect storm – an antagonistic government; free licences for the over 75s; a vociferous loyal base complaining at cuts; a significant section of their funders (young people) who pay but don't use and who might not want to pay; and Netflix, Amazon, Disney, Apple, YouTube and a few others. Not a storm easily endured.

Now, all this may change in the present maelstrom of contemporaneous life. Initially, lockdown helped mainstream broadcasters in general, and the BBC and its news services in particular, as they all seemed to enjoy significantly increased viewing.

That may have changed as the lockdown went on, as anecdotal evidence was that the non-stop diet of unending bad news put media users off – an issue that was relevant to print as well. But there were questions about the quality of journalism on show, especially at the televised Downing Street briefings that helped no-one.

And print, and its associated online commercial market, suffering during lockdown, too. Single copy sales were in freefall as readers stayed at home; advertising plunged; digital advertisers wished to go nowhere near Covid stories; both nationals and regionals furloughed staff. It wasn't and isn't good.

No-one can offer a realistic prediction of where this may all end up – but what is for sure is that the basic issues facing both traditional broadcasters, and specifically the BBC, and print will not be disappearing, whatever the outcome of the pandemic.

The good old days

But, back to BC – Before Coronavirus. Print in the early 2000s had not a bad reader base still, but was propped up by jobs advertising. The BBC in the late 2010s had not a bad viewing/listening base still, but was propped up by the licence fee.

But what questions link them?

The first, and most important of these, is audience. Broadly, newspapers sales (along with, significantly, readership) across both national and regional sectors has been declining since the early 1970s. There have been notable exceptions, but the overall curve has moved just one way.

Traditional television viewing has shown a similar trajectory since the early 2000s with the rise of YouTube, Netflix and the many other on-demand services that have launched, so dampening the brand loyalty and recognition that the BBC and ITV (and Channel 4 latterly) enjoyed in a reasonably unfettered way from the late 1950s onwards for 40 plus years.

This was recognised in TV land, but was it taken seriously? In October, 2001 Richard Deverell, then Head of Strategy at BBC News, told a gathering of newspaper editors: "We'd give anything to enjoy your relatively slow rates of [print] audience decline." [Our research indicates] that 17 million people, a third of the entire UK population, watch at least one edition of the Nine o'clock news each week. However, only 200,000 people watch all five a week."

Essentially newspaper readers and legacy television viewers have followed the same paths, albeit with a 20-year lag. Newspaper readers found different things to do; BBC viewers have done the same. And there is evidence that legacy television bosses might be trailing the same decision-making route as newspaper managements.

Every year, regional print readership would decline and ad rates (especially those for sits vac) would ascend. There wasn't much debate about how to keep existing readers onside and to attract and retain new readers for the long term.

Is the BBC following a well-trod path here? It's cutting costs for its core audience (does it not understand that diehards appreciate, for example, what is behind a cut-down version of Clive Anderson's *Loose Ends* on Radio 4 at 1130am on a Monday?) and that audience doesn't like it.

It is piling money in to its Sounds app in an attempt to attract a hard-to-find current-day young demographic while disenchanting its main flag-wavers. And once those key supporters have left the room, as newspapers know to their cost, they are desperately difficult to entice back.

Now newspaper managements will argue their titles have never been seen by more readers than now because of digital uptake, but it is inarguable that advertising yields have plummeted, online reading spans are shorter and cost pressures have intensified.

For ITV, Channel 4 and Channel 5 the issues are the same as for newspapers. Viewers are going to other suppliers; advertisers are getting less for their money; a desperate search is on for a solution.

But for the BBC the problem is different because of its funding mechanism. Justifying the licence in a changed world to the population at large – especially the groups who live outside London, or who are young and don't use much, if any, of its services – remains a significant task.

Other similarities

But is it not just audience where there are similarities. Other areas where regional print went wrong are relevant.

The regional and local newspaper sector did not research the future. During the golden years of high profits between 1989 and 2005 it could have looked ahead but failed to do so. *Did the BBC do the same when viewing was high and the growth of new digital devices was in its infancy?*

Regional press did not understand its customer base sufficiently. It looked at how its customers interacted with the newspaper products themselves but did not look at how their lifestyles were changing until it was too late. *Surely the same for the BBC?*

Regional and local groups failed to experiment as the shifting market place became apparent. Different business models could have been tried. They weren't. *Could the BBC not have put forward ideas such as BritBox when Netflix was new, rather than now, when it is arguably years too late.*

Senior executives in the regions were viewed by their staffs, both senior and junior, as being too focused on the bottom line. They did not believe it would end. They did not see that the Internet would merely conclude what had been happening for decades. *Again, is this not the same for BBC senior executives over the years? 'We're wonderful; everyone loves us; it's only 150 quid or so; why can't it go on?'*

And there were individual broadcasting signs that the BBC perhaps pushed to one side, but were all coming together, slowly.

The launch of satellite broadcasting in 1983; the merger of Sky and BSB in 1990; the decline in mass viewing from the heady days of Morecambe and Wise Christmas specials (Little and Large were dumped by the BBC in 1991, allegedly, for attracting only eight million viewers to their last series – today eight million is deemed a major success); the steady movement of sports, one by one, to other channels; the growth of social media.

All these gradually played a part in moving the BBC away from being the pinnacle of the nation's cultural pyramid. Individually not over important, together a toxic recipe for disaster.

And is it continuing? Is there too much naval gazing? Does the BBC see life too much through London eyes and does this just amplify the belief that core audiences have been ignored by out-of-touch executives?

However, no-one on any side of the regional print debate has been able to say with any certainty what could have been done differently to prevent the advertising model changing so radically with the Internet. Local newspapers may well be a victim of an unstoppable alliance of a changed socio-economic environment and advanced technology.

And in general terms is this the same for the BBC? Could it have reinvented itself as a Sky or a Netflix – or is so wedded to the licence-fee model that change on a radical scale was never going to be possible? Or full stop, the BBC may also be a potential victim of an alternative unstoppable alliance.

It is in a crisis that has been long in the making, and not just one that appeared when Boris Johnson won his landslide in December. The causes for concern have been visible in clear sight but have been roundly ignored. Sounds very similar to the regional and local press to me. Welcome to our world.

About the writer

Neil Fowler is co-editor of this book. This chapter is based on an article that first appeared in *InPublshing* magazine.

Sarah Greene, presenter, *Blue Peter*, 1980-83; *Saturday Superstore*, 1983-87; *Going Live*, 1980-93

If I'm correct that the lost generation is truly considered to be the entire audience under 30, then my initial reaction would be to ask how on earth anyone – whether they are part of a corporation, or are a service provider, a commissioner, a producer, a scheduler, a writer, a director, a performer – could consider this to be one generation? With a one-approach-fits-all answer?

The reasons as to why this huge span of an audience with vastly different needs has apparently moved away are, I'm sure, many and varied. Perhaps the answer is that it was never there.

The BBC devolved its children's department to CBeebies and CBBC 18 years ago. Anyone who was around eight or 10 at the time and used to being a member of a much bigger audience of both younger and, significantly, adult viewers might have baulked at the idea of being hived off and categorised as somehow 'other'. Of course audience loyalty has to start with the quality of the output, but it's also about habit. Once the habit is lost...

In the 1980s and early 1990s the BBC cherished its children's department. The erstwhile charismatic controller of BBC 2, Aubrey Singer, referred to it as 'the jewel in the BBC's crown'.

Here was a man who, like others of his generation of BBC management, realised the blindingly obvious: you have to grow your audience. You have to carefully invest in inclusively nurturing an audience from a young age. That way you'll have a better chance of keeping them.

Then there are the programmes which, although intended for one age group, really do manage to appeal across the generations. Ironically, Going Live *was criticised at the time (BBC 1 Saturday mornings, three hours live, 1987-1993) by some within the BBC of having a massive audience aged between 16-30...they would dream of that now!*

Compounding the fragmentation from within the BBC itself, there followed the digital revolution and its resulting explosion of channels and choice. If the BBC habit was in danger of being forgotten by young people nearly 20 years ago, then there were hundreds of new and exciting ways to fill the gap.

The sad thing is, the BBC's commitment to making great programmes for children is still there and the opportunities for inclusion and interaction are better than ever – but the enjoyment of 'belonging' and being part of a much bigger audience has to be rediscovered. If it can be, perhaps in about 20 years the 30-year-olds will be part of a found generation.

Chapter 17

The *Sesame Street* effect. What it means for UK broadcasters and their black and Asian audiences

UK broadcasters are losing their BAME (Black, Asian and Minority Ethnic) audiences because they are valuing individual characters and actors instead of championing rich diverse communities – a lesson one of the most influential of children's programmes learnt 50 years ago. Marcus Ryder explains

There is no doubt that British broadcasting is some of the best in the world. I love a lot of the programmes the BBC, ITV, Channel 4 and Channel 5 produce. But the truth is, as a black person, on an emotional level, the BBC and the other broadcasters lost me the year before I was even born.

The year was 1970. That year *Sesame Street* launched, with an opening scene of a black male teacher in a suit, walking a young black girl, Sally, down the street and introducing her to a multicultural neighbourhood. They walk to his home and he introduces her to his black wife who gives Sally cookies and milk.

From the very first frame, *Sesame Street* put an aspirational, professional black couple at the heart of its programme. And by doing so, it captured my heart.

In contrast, during the 1970s, on a Saturday morning I would flick between *Multi-Coloured Swap Shop'* and *Tiswas* but neither had my undying loyalty. I was neither a *Blue Peter* nor even a *Magpie* child, the two flagship children's programmes of BBC or ITV respectively.

Despite being born and raised in London I looked across the Atlantic and saw myself reflected back at me and in a reality I wanted to be part of. I looked at programmes filmed just down the road from where I lived and failed to find an emotional connection.

I had no conscious understanding of race but something in *Sesame Street* resonated with me. It got something right in 1970 which British television still fails to grasp.

Over the last 50 years there has been real progress, with most British drama writers now recognising that there should be positive black characters. Casting directors are now more willing to cast black actors in non-stereotypical positive roles. Things are far from perfect, but there is no denying that progression. We see positive black characters on our screen relatively often – from actors in *Dr Who* to *The Hustle* and of course *Luther*. However, there's something special about these positive characters.

How communities are portrayed

They are often the only black character, inhabiting functioning white communities, or at the very least majority white communities. Black communities on TV on the other hand are portrayed almost exclusively as dysfunctional. While many of the people portrayed in a drama set in a BAME community may be likable, the community they were set in is normally anything but.

The message that comes across loud and clear on our screens is that while there might be good black individuals, black communities are a problem. It suggests that if you are a good or positive black person you should want to leave the dysfunctional black communities as quickly as possible.

While some might downplay these unspoken messages, the reality is one comes across these implicit negative views about black communities all the time. There are often similar messages about South Asians on TV, while there might be positive individuals from the Indian sub-continent, the communities are invariably problematic, populated with forced marriages and potential terrorists. And unfortunately, in the UK, East Asian representation is still so thin on the ground it is almost impossible to discuss it sensibly.

Yet the reality is that while dysfunctional black communities certainly do exist, there are also incredibly good positive functional communities. Analysis by Dr Nicola Rollock into the black middle class offers strong examples of functional positive black communities that rarely see our TV screens. I for one am very proud to be part of a black community that includes lawyers, film makers, policemen, civil servants, charity workers – but also unemployed people. It's mixed, but positively so.

British public service broadcasters (PSBs) are on the edge of a precipice. In 2018 the media regulator Ofcom warned that they were at risk of losing a generation of viewers, as younger audiences under 30 turned away from the traditional broadcasters and opted to watch Netflix, Amazon and other SVODs (subscription video on demand) instead, as well as other online content.

Also, according to another recent report by the UK media regulator, when it comes to diversity British audiences are increasingly finding better representation and authentic portrayal on Netflix and other online video-streaming providers. Every executive I speak to at a PSB is aware of these statistics and recognises the need to address them.

However, in my experience they do not fully grasp the problem facing them with regards to BAME viewers. They know the BAME viewing figures are worse than their white equivalents but they normally just attribute this to the fact that the BAME community is proportionately younger than the overall white UK population and just see it as part of the wider problem of losing their younger audience.

However, I believe the problem is far deeper than this.

In the 1970s I might not have been in love with the BBC or ITV and I might have wished I lived on *Sesame Street* but, with only three terrestrial channels, I was stuck in the UK. There was no way I could move to the functional beautiful multicultural neighbourhood populated with black teachers and children that looked just like me.

But now, in 2020, our younger children can move to *Sesame Street* whenever they want. And our older children can see aspirational black communities on HBO's *Insecure* or ABC's *Black-ish*. So why aren't these positive, broader messages about our diverse communities coming out on UK PSBs?

What Netflix is getting right

Why have online providers been able to learn from the lessons of *Sesame Street* and build upon them while legacy broadcasters like the BBC, ITV and Channel 4, still seem to be failing their ethnically diverse audiences?

Are the executives and commissioners at the SVODs and online providers more enlightened and receptive to diversity compared to their counterparts at the BBC, ITV, Channel 4 and Channel 5?

While people are important, I very much doubt that the difference can be attributed to just the different attitudes of a few individuals and commissioners. For one thing many of the commissioners and senior gatekeepers at the SVODs are from the PSBs originally and flip back and forth between the different types of broadcasters.

Instead, I believe the answer can be found in the different economic models between traditional broadcasters versus online video streamers.

Amanda Lotz, a professor of media studies at the University of Michigan, analysed Netflix's economic model in 2017 and argued that traditional broadcasters still think in terms of attracting large audiences for a single programme as advertisers pay for eyeballs. As an American she didn't look at the BBC but I would argue the same argument applies as the BBC still looks to large audiences to justify its licence fee.

Online streamers like Netflix and Amazon – on the other hand – are not pursuing large audiences for advertisers. Instead, they are trying to maximize subscribers.

Quoted in *The Conversation*, Professor Lotz says: "To succeed, subscriber-funded services must offer enough programming that viewers find the service worthy of their monthly fee. Each show doesn't need a mass audience – which is the measure of success for advertiser-funded television – but the service does need to provide enough value that subscribers continue to pay."

Professor Lotz describes the strategy Netflix employs as 'conglomerated niche' and says that because it does not broadcast in a linear fashion most subscribers don't even know most of Netflix's content and only concentrate on the series that appeal to them.

She uses the metaphor of a library to describe this phenomenon: "If you were to ask different Netflix subscribers about the service's brand, you'd likely get different responses. There is no one Netflix; rather, think of it as an expansive library with many small nooks and rooms. Most subscribers never wander floor to floor. Instead, they stay in the corner that matches their tastes."

The strength of niche audiences

This means channel executives at traditional broadcasters think completely differently when it comes to commissioning content versus commissioners at Netflix. The BBC executive, for example, is thinking: "Will the programme get a large audience?" while the Netflix executive is thinking: "Will this new series be able to get a new different section of the audience to subscribe?"

The Netflix execs are constantly seeking out programmes that will get a different niche audience to subscribe or continue to subscribe.

Take my favourite series at the moment *Insecure*, which I mentioned earlier. It finally tipped the balance for me to finally take out a subscription for HBO Go and I am sure I am not the only one. '*Insecure*' is therefore a win for HBO, in a way that commissioning yet another 'non-diverse' programme would not be, as it wouldn't attract new subscribers.

Compare this to ITV or BBC. All things being equal the ITV and BBC commissioners would prefer to commission another series like *Call the Midwife* as it would bring in a far larger audience, even if it is the same old non-diverse audience that already watches the majority of their programmes, than commission *Insecure,* which relatively speaking would be a ratings flop.

Television executives could even make *Call the Midwife* more ethnically diverse by adding a few Caribbean nurses. This is the type of diversity that is often favoured by executives as it broadens the programme's appeal without risking the core audience. However, this approach does not address the fundamental *Sesame Street* strategy of creating a community.

For this reason, the SVODs approach leads to far deeper diverse programmes being commissioned by broadcasters who are financed by subscribers. The irony is that in targeting niche audiences streaming services often create quality content, which over time has a far wider appeal.

If you talk to executives of traditional broadcasters they all recognise the importance of commissioning for non-linear viewing and targeting certain demographics. But it is still incredibly hard for commissioners to break out of a linear 'big-audiences-matter' state of mind.

The truth is as traditional broadcasters worry about big audiences now, they risk having no audiences in the future. Only by recognizing the rich diversity of their audiences, and creating programmes that they want to watch, will broadcasters survive. *Sesame Street* may have been launched in a time before SVODs but its entire model has been based around this idea.

Just two years after *Sesame Street* began in America it launched a Brazilian version. Importantly, it did not simply dub the American version into Portuguese or add a few Brazilian characters. It relocated into a new community that reflected Brazil's diversity.

It has repeated the same trick in at least 34 different countries including South Africa, Russia, Palestine and Israel. Interestingly, the UK broadcasters consistently rejected working with the producers of *Sesame Street* and so there was never a British version I could identify with. Instead I fell in love with the American one.

I will leave you with one more *Sesame Street*-related fact.

When the first episode of *Sesame Street* was aired in 1970 the US was 87.65 per cent white. According to the last census conducted in 2010 it is now 72.40 per cent white.

The year I was born, 1971, was the first time the UK census specifically gathered ethnicity data. That year they found the white population made up roughly 97.7 per cent of the population. Today the BAME population in the UK is 13 per cent, a larger percentage than the non-white US population at the time Sally first met all the *Sesame Street* characters in the first episode.

In 1970 a children's television show had already worked out the importance of appealing to the country's non-white population, an appeal that made a small child born in London a year later fall in love with it.

British broadcasters do not have the luxury of waiting another 50 years to finally work out what *Sesame Street* got right. Because unlike 50 years ago *Sesame Street* is literally just one channel hop away, as is all the other great diverse content that prioritises community representation over simple diverse representation of individuals.

About the writer

Marcus Ryder is an award-winning executive producer at Caixin Global, China's leading financial publication. He is a visiting professor in media diversity at Birmingham City University and was a core member of the executive committee to launch the Sir Lenny Henry Centre for Media Diversity.

He has worked in television for more than 25 years. For eight years he oversaw BBC Scotland's current affairs documentaries where he formulated his ideas on the importance of diverse representation championing communities as opposed to simply increasing the representation of different types of individuals.

169

Chapter 18

Fundamental change must access all areas

Legacy systems and infrastructure need not hold back traditional broadcasters in the battle with new players, says RTÉ's Richard Waghorn, but agility, vision and determination are required

As with every other industry the internet continues to fundamentally change the traditional broadcast business:

- consumers are increasingly using fixed and mobile broadband to access TV channels and video content;
- on-demand is diminishing linear TV's historic importance;
- apps, playlists and smart speakers are displacing the role of electronic programme guides;
- social media, rather than the watercooler, is the new home for recommendations with a user's social media networks offering opinions on what to watch.

The internet has enabled the growth of over-the-top (OTT) video and audio services with new business models with many operating on a global scale. As green field entrants, the OTT players don't have legacy broadcast infrastructures, systems and workflows to deal with, and they have been able to achieve significant international reach and scale without the same regulatory conditions that are placed on national public service broadcasters.

As a result of this fundamental change, younger audiences are engaging with media in different ways. Not only are they consuming more with the increased choice on offer, but they have developed new ways of consuming; not just on multiple different devices, in any location, and at any time of the day, but by being able to easily skip through content and ads, binge-view, interact on social media while watching (double screening), and create and share their own content. The under-30s don't have experience of a world without the internet, so they expect a great dynamic user experience, and preferably one that is personalised to them.

The lost generation is not fully lost to PSBs

Younger generations have developed a voracious appetite for content and they know how to seek it out. They are looking for more than what public service broadcasters (PSBs) can offer alone on their linear broadcast channels and broadcaster video-on-demand services (BVOD). Whilst OTT players offer global hits such as *Tiger King* and *The Crown*, they also enable access to a wide range of niche content, and do this all on a global scale, curating and dubbing the content for different territories, and making it easy to search and discover.

Younger audiences know what they want and despite the plethora of choice they know how to find it. Whatever their specific or niche interests there is content out there on the internet to satisfy their needs.

Whilst the under-30s audience consumes less PSB content than the generations before them, they still consume PSB content – so they are not fully lost.

PSBs (including the BBC) are trying to extend their reach and appeal to young audiences through all their platforms. With BBC Three, both in its linear and online forms, the BBC has had huge success with shows such as *Little Britain*, *Gavin and Stacey*, *Two Pints of Lager*, and more recently with programming as varied as *Fleabag*, *Killing Eve*, *People Just Do Nothing*, *RuPaul's Drag Race UK* and *Normal People*, all of which have a strong following and have resonated heavily with the under-30s.

Young audiences are not resistant to linear broadcast as it is still the dominant home for live and topical programming, such as live news and sport, as well as entertainment and reality shows, such as ITV's *I'm a Celebrity* and *Love Island*.

Indeed, at the time of writing, the BBC in its annual plan is even considering a return to linear broadcast for a revitalised BBC Three, fueled by its recent hits.

Taking an example from Ireland, about a third of 15-34s watching linear TV at 6pm and 9pm are watching the news on RTÉ One, despite the distraction of all the OTT players and several hundred other linear TV channels (RTÉ is a public broadcaster in the Republic of Ireland). In addition, young audiences are still accessing RTÉ's content through radio, RTÉ.ie, the News Now app and social media platforms. There are multiple touch points, and the challenge is to ensure that those connections with the under-30s are maintained and built on, whilst balancing that with the need to maintain appeal with older audience groups.

Yes, it's all about the content...

In order to be more attractive to the younger generations, PSBs need to ensure that content is relevant and can easily be found and enjoyed. Easier said than done. Other chapters in this book discuss the challenges around funding, resourcing and producing relevant content and the need to take calculated risks with commissioning.

However, one of the biggest challenges for PSBs is funding and ensuring that funds are efficiently used. A key objective is to ensure that as much funding as possible can be freed up to support the making, marketing and distribution of content, and to enable staff to be more creative and efficient in making content for younger audiences. And that is where technology and operations can help.

...but it's also about technology and operations

Given the PSBs' history, most carry the legacy of their broadcast-only adolescence – technology environments, studio facilities, production models, workflows, and work practices – which means that they are not as technically agile as OTT players. PSBs also operate many services and are often obliged to offer them across a wide variety of platforms. Also, PSBs produce a significant volume of live programming and need the infrastructure and capability to support that.

The ability to be agile and flexible and to be able to rapidly scale to meet fast-changing demands is a challenge when dealing with legacy issues and brownfield environments. It's not an unsurmountable challenge, but it takes clear vision, determined leadership and considerable time and money to transform technology environments and operational practices.

The prize is to deliver a flexible, agile and scalable production, broadcast and distribution business, delivering cost savings and operational efficiencies that can be harvested into creating more content and offering a great user experience – vital for the under-30 audience.

There are a number of aspects to how RTÉ is transforming its technology and operations to help unlock value for the whole business and its audiences, and this provides a framework for others:

- **Embracing cloud and IP technologies and optimising core technology**. RTÉ has adopted a hybrid cloud strategy (private and public), enhanced storage capabilities, significantly increased internal and external network capacity, built-in improved resilience in critical areas, enforced IT security and access controls, and rationalised the application footprint.

- **Modernising production and broadcast facilities and workflows**. RTÉ is completing its migration to file-based working across all areas of the business, has upgraded studios, post-production and playout (to HD and UHD as appropriate), and built new flexible, automated studios that can be rapidly turned around for different productions.

- **Expanding remote and lightweight production capabilities**. RTÉ was an early adopter of MoJo (mobile journalism) using mobile devices for creating, editing and distributing content, and continues to exploit IP, cloud and mobile technologies to enable more flexible, timely and cost-effective production from any location using fewer resources.

- **Empowering productivity and collaboration**. RTÉ uses standardised off-the-shelf systems and tools (for example cloud-based email, communications, storage, collaboration platforms) to facilitate staff and teams to adopt new digital ways of working and develop more efficient workflows. In reacting to Covid-19, there has been a significant uptake and adoption of this toolset and as a result a number of manual and paper workflows have been eliminated for good.

- **Unlocking the value of data**. Business areas across RTÉ are adopting data strategies to get better insights on audience engagement and operational performance. RTÉ has developed new workflows and taxonomies to support the cataloguing and tagging of content, aiding search, navigation and personalisation.

- **Designing exceptional user experiences**. Digital products need to have strong designs, be simple to use, and be feature rich (such as live re-start, downloads for offline consumption, integration with other devices and personalised recommendations).

This is the journey of travel that RTÉ is on and whilst good progress has been made we are not fully there (just yet).

What RTÉ is doing is embracing cloud and IP technologies to transform its business and its operations to ensure that it is competitive with the OTT operators and to ensure it is best placed to attract young audiences. This should be the objective of every PSB.

Delivering results

RTÉ is already seeing the benefits of the approach it is taking, and I would argue that this is helping to contribute to RTÉ attracting the under-30s audiences to its content. For example:

The new flexible studios that have been built have enabled us to increase the production quality of programmes and have given production teams new ways of telling stories with higher quality graphics and augmented reality, and at a lower cost.

With the investments in our infrastructure, we have been able to improve the picture quality of our video content from glass-to-glass offering a higher quality experience across broadcast and digital platforms.

The investments we have made in back-end systems and processes has enabled better alignment and integration between the linear channels and the player supporting cross-scheduling and promotions.

Our adoption of mobile bonding and IP audio codec technologies has enabled more flexibility in the production space and gives production teams more creative latitude.

RTÉ is achieving this against reduced investment budgets while containing its spend on technology operational costs – as a proportion of total costs spend on technology remains about 3 per cent, but now, we have increased our technical capability. Across the entire business, operational efficiencies are being delivered enabling content teams to produce and serve a greater volume of content across multiple platforms.

Just as the internet has fundamentally changed the media market, PSBs need to fundamentally change their technology and operations to ensure that they can remain competitive. PSBs need to transform their legacy environments to make them flexible and agile and easily scalable so that they can easily respond to the demands of younger audiences now and in the future.

About the writer

Richard Waghorn is Director of Operations, Technology and Transformation at Raidió Teilifís Éireann (RTÉ) in the Republic of Ireland. He has 25 years' experience of driving performance, efficiency and digital transformation for major media organisations, including RTÉ, the BBC and South Africa's SABC. At RTÉ, Richard has restructured the technology function, increased the market share of Saorview, (Ireland's free-to-air digital television platform), and is leading a programme of organisational transformation. A former member of the European Broadcasting Union's Technical Committee, Richard is currently a member of the IBC Council.

At the SABC, Richard led the technology division holding the strategic and operational leadership of the digital agenda, TV and radio production facilities, outside broadcasts and IT. He led major digital and infrastructure projects, and drove operational efficiencies.

At the BBC, Richard led the distribution business unit which delivered universal access to television, radio and digital services on broadcast platforms. He led the BBC's involvement in the national digital switchover programme and was a board director of Freesat. Prior to this, Richard was the project manager for the launch of Freeview in 2002.

Chapter 19

Game-changing attitudes?

Whilst a narrative exists that the BBC is wholly failing to engage with the next generation, there is at least one part of the corporation where success in attracting and retaining the sought-after youth audience has been achieved. That's sport, says Marc Webber

The accusation that the BBC does not understand 18-24-year-olds has developed through media coverage of the issue and through a gloom-laden report by the UK regulator, Ofcom. The major sentence in that report of October 2019 stated: "The BBC may not be sustainable in its current form, if it fails to regain younger audiences who are increasingly tuning out of its services."

The Achilles heel in this narrative is two-fold and BBC Sport is challenging this on both linear platforms and in the new worlds of social and digital media.

Firstly, the Ofcom report cited a dip in linear BBC TV viewing of 50 per cent by that age group as the reason the broadcaster was at risk. What the Ofcom report failed to recognise is this is less of a concern when it comes to BBC sport output on television.

BBC Sport on linear television is largely powered by 'appointment-to-view' TV – that is, live sport or live sport discussion shows with content that has immediate currency. This gives it more value for any audience, let alone a younger one, as the need to know now is a common social need for any age group.

If you do not think young people do not crave to be clued up on live events, ask yourself why the trending sections of social platforms are such a powerful tool for younger-skewed social platforms?

BBC Sport has retained its strength in that area despite an expensive rights market and has diversified the BBC's audience through the power of live sport by adding disciplines not previously available in a pre-digital or multi-channel world.

The red button is now shorthand for live sport in the minds of many consumers of BBC content. The streamed sports offered by the BBC may seem like they are there because the rights are cheap/free, and no one wants them. But there is a conscious effort behind-the-scenes at BBC Sport to use its public service remit to show sports that attract a younger, diverse audience which can also have traction on social and video-sharing platforms.

The soon-to-be Olympic sport of speed climbing and the 2019 World Urban Games – which consisted of basketball 3x3s and Parkour – gained extensive coverage on BBC sport, with live streams and blogs, coupled with the more viral elements shared through Twitter and Instagram.

A change in tone

And think of the way BBC Sport's marketing tone has switched in the past few years. The best example of this would be its 2019 *Change the Game* ad campaign to promote a summer of women's elite sport. It wasn't just a campaign led by women to tell you there would be lots of women's sport on. The stars were young, diverse sporting heroines – the current generation to inspire the next generation. Its production was edgy, attention-grabbing and in your face. Just what the 'lost' generation expect.

BBC Sport may also have weapon from its past, which could help attract the younger audiences of now. It is something that goes against the common trajectory of heritage media brands, which tend to struggle with engaging a new generation. You only have to look to the field of news, where long-standing newspaper titles have fought against the brave new charges of *Huffington Post* to see it is harder to hold.

Or, how about looking at the internal BBC example of this?

Top of the Pops (TOTP) was *the* music television brand in the UK for more than three decades. Generations of young people got their musical education from *TOTP* either on TV, radio or in print.

Both *Top of the Pops* and BBC Sport came under their first waves of attack in the early 90s, when the likes of MTV, VH1 and Sky Sports started eating away at the younger demographic. But the real killer for TOTP came in the 2000s, when nascent mp3 download services like Napster and, eventually, YouTube became the cool way to consume music.

Contrast this with the fate of BBC Sport's most renowned subbrand, *Match of the Day (MOTD)*.

It too was under attack from a growth live TV channels and numerous sports websites like Teamtalk, plus social media channels like Sport Bible, actual teams, players, fans and sponsors who now have their own voice on social media (more on these later).

However, the difference here is that the *MOTD* audience base might have been more age-diverse from the start than *TOTP*, giving it more of an ability to branch out into innovations and get a firmer grip on the lost generations.

TOTP was not aiming for a family audience -it wanted a young audience. *MOTD* always attracted a family audience, whether that be a Saturday night treat for children to stay up and watch it with their parents, or them watch it together during the early Sunday morning repeat.

BBC Sport insiders believe the talent which fronts *MOTD* and other live sport shows is respected by all age groups. And now, the presentation roster is younger and more diverse, audience research suggests to BBC insiders that whilst they can often be the subject of a Twitter storm for employing 'squeaky-voiced female commentators' or 'showbiz pundits', those are straw men compared to the positive focus-group feedback they receive from the younger demographic the BBC desperately courts.

Influencing the airwaves

With the feeling the core product is accessible to all, BBC Sport has felt more able to take creative risks to lock down audience growth from an early age through its spin-off shows, starting with *MOTD Kickabout* for children and the recently-launched *MOTDx*, which nakedly aims for that increasingly lucrative ground where football playing meets off-the-pitch culture, fashion and music.

It is a show that attracts the right audience in the right way and is, perhaps, a great example of the thinking behind-the-scenes at BBC Sport, which has attracted a younger demographic to the output.

"You have to look for talent where your audience is," a BBC producer once told me. Sounds a simple concept, but it has proven to be a controversial one in some parts.

BBC sport's audience research in the initial drive for 18-24-year-olds showed this audience was attracted to people who were not visible on their current output. People like Spencer FC, Arsenal Fan TV and football podcasters were the people grabbing the audience and holding it on other platforms.

BBC Sport was one of the earliest adopters of embedding these influencers into its content. Whether that be inviting the Fulham FC fans podcast, *Fulhamish*, to predict the weekend's scores on the website, or giving a podcast to footballer *Peter*

Crouch – a crazy, on-the-fly, low-budget idea which has now become an aural behemoth. It has been downloaded 12m times over three series and is now a 2.01m-high tentpole in the sports provision of the BBC's nascent podcast platform, BBC Sounds.

By deciding to integrate influencers throughout all its content, one digital media expert believes it has stolen a march on other traditional broadcasters.

"The way they latched on to influencers very early has been a major boost for them. There was definitely a risk that BBC Sport could have looked jaded to younger audiences. But they seemed to understand earlier than other traditional media that there was this other world out there and they needed to inject some of that into their output," says Dan McLaren, a sports social media consultant with more than a decade of experience, now working with SQN Agency, which lists digital clients such as Williams F1 and Henley Regatta amongst others.

But, there is a schism with this policy which has caused controversy. Finding influencers and younger talent has attracted the wrath of mainstream media who believe the BBC is ditching older, more experienced sports journalists for childish banter-based content with little informative value.

There is no more obvious an example of this battle is being played out than on Radio 5 Live, where the station has courted media wrath for its 'dumping' of award-winning stalwarts such as Gary Richardson's *Sportsweek* show and revered Mark Pougatch for millennial football podcasters like *The Squad*, which has come under attack for lacking insight and, at times, for being hard to listen to.

One harsh review of the podcast said: "This is hard work to listen to. It's like being trapped inside a kebab shop at 3am in the morning with a bunch of incoherent drunks all shouting at each other about football."

Radio 5 Live would say it is not about enhancing coverage for one underserved audience to the detriment of another. Changes to talent rota have been commonplace in its history – and similar media outrage often followed before fading into the atmosphere like a late-night medium-wave signal.

Bowling them over

Critics such as *The Guardian's* Sarah Manavis use the fact the BBC has not officially launched itself onto TikTok – the latest social network de rigeur – as evidence that the corporation is failing its younger audience. But the approach behind the scenes is not to rush onto the latest platform just to be seen there. It is more about flexibility with the right content, on the right platform at the right time.

BBC Sport has a younger audience champion. A staff member who sits at the heart of the operation and ensures everyone in the team understands the DNA of this demographic. They are there as a sense check, using data to share understanding of what works where in a world where this audience expect your content to be like the old Martini television ad suggested – consumable anytime, anyplace, anywhere.

It is all about working out what delivers engagement on individual platforms and what connections you can make with content and users already gaining traction on those platforms.

The best example of that was when the BBC made bowls sexy. A fantastic shot (or good wood as bowlers call it) by Nick Brett at the World Championships in January 2020 doesn't instantly stand out as viral content to be shared by the 'yoof'.

But those running the social channels knew the simple mantra of social media – good content flies. Even an 18-year-old 'lad' in North London would share this act of sporting skill from a game stereotypically viewed by an older audience. And so it was, as there were 1.5m views in the first day alone on the BBC's iPlayer, and the clip was also widely shared on numerous other sites and social media accounts worldwide.

You will notice the tone and structure on a BBC Sport Instagram post is different from a Twitter post – but both get similar levels of engagement. The *MOTD* Twitter feed is more conversational than the BBC sport feed – except, perhaps, during matchdays where game facts are still craved by a generation that supposedly are more susceptible to ingest fake news.

All BBC accounts are not afraid to share TikTok videos or other media posted by players or events. This again proves why BBC Sport has done well with younger audiences, by admitting when others make better content and being part of the sharing conversation, as opposed to leading it.

In conclusion, it is BBC Sport's mix of evergreen heritage brands, early understanding of influencer power and knowledge of what content works where, which has made them win over a larger proportion of a younger audience than other areas of the business. Surely anyone that can make bowls go viral must be doing something right?

References

Sarah Manavis: "Why the BBC is so bad at engaging younger audiences" *Guardian* online
https://www.theguardian.com/commentisfree/2020/jan/28/bbc-younger-audience-youtube-tiktok-social-media (accessed 21 May 2020)
Ofcom: Second Annual Report on the BBC, published October 2019
https://www.Ofcom.org.uk/__data/assets/pdf_file/0026/173735/second-bbc-annual-report.pdf (accessed 21 May 2020)
BBC coverage of 2019 Speed Climbing World Championships
https://www.bbc.co.uk/programmes/p07kjc2h (page accessed 21 May 2020)
BBC coverage of the 2019 World Urban Games
https://www.bbc.co.uk/sport/49653891 (page accessed 21 May 2020)
BBC media centre release on Change the Game campaign 01 May 2019.
https://www.bbc.co.uk/mediacentre/mediapacks/change-the-game
TOTP archive page on BBC http://www.bbc.co.uk/totp/history/
2019 BBC Sounds podcasting figures released to Radio Today
https://radiotoday.co.uk/2019/12/record-podcast-listening-reported-by-bbc-sounds-in-2019/

SQN AGENCY WEBSITE https://sqn.agency/
Telegraph article on criticism of closure of Gary Richardson's *Sportsweek* (16 Sept 2019)
https://www.telegraph.co.uk/sport/2019/09/16/bbc-stands-firm-sportsweek-radio-show-axing-despite-outcry-public/
Daily Mail article on Mark Pougatch leaving Radio 5
https://www.dailymail.co.uk/news/article-8299981/BBC-Sport-boss-defends-cull-veteran-broadcasters.html
Podcast reviews for *The Squad*
https://chartable.com/podcasts/the-squad/reviews
1980s Martini Ad
https://www.youtube.com/watch?v=6L6CbIR0Pkw
BBC sport Bowls World Championship shot.
https://www.bbc.co.uk/sport/av/51207174
Potters story about views for Bowls shot.
https://www.pottersholidays.com/post/article/world-bowls-goes-viral

About the writer

Marc Webber is currently course leader of the BA(Hons) Multimedia Sports Journalism at the University of Northampton. The course is recognised by the Broadcast Journalism Training Council.

Marc's career as a sports journalist stretches over nearly three decades. Starting as a match reporter on Welsh domestic football in 1992, Marc has gone on to report on most sports for media as diverse as the *Financial Times* to *When Saturday Comes* magazine.

His first experience of digital journalism came in when he was part of the launch team producing online video news content for the Press Association. He went on to win awards for online video at *The Sun* and an ARIA audio award as part of the audioBoom podcast hosting team.

He is a match day reporter for BBC's *Final Score* show and does this as well as present the Northampton Town football programme on Radio Northampton. Contacts: https://www.linkedin.com/in/marcwebber/ and on Twitter at @marcwebber

Vox Populi

Ruthie Matthewson, 27, tax adviser, London

Any BBC content I access is live – I rarely use iPlayer. In terms of television content, I look to BBC One or BBC Three for live entertainment/news. Generally, my BBC listening experiences are limited to Radio 1 (in the car) or Radio 3 (on a Sunday afternoon with a glass of red).

I rely on the BBC, as a trusted broadcaster, to provide (what I view to be) an unbiased and accurate presentation of world news.

The BBC should definitely get rid of a few channels/shows. Does anyone really need to see another episode of Eggheads*? And plug the savings into BBC original dramas and more sports.*

The BBC sometimes doesn't market itself very well – it needs bigger advertising campaigns. There are so many great shows on the BBC that I only ever hear about because someone has recommended them. I rarely see adverts on my social media or on the tube.

The BBC is quintessentially British, with great variety and quality. It has strong news/sports coverage and some surprisingly good series such as The Thick of It, Peaky Blinders *and* Line of Duty.

Chapter 20

Just a few ideas lying around...

It's an overflowing in-tray on the incoming Director-General's desk. Michael Wilson explores the priorities set out by contributors to this book and adds a few throughs of his own

The Economist Milton Freidman is once said: "Only a crisis – actual or perceived – produces real change. When a crisis occurs, the actions that are taken depend on the ideas that are lying around."

So expect change soon at the BBC.

And I do hope this book may be lying around. There are certainly more good ideas from the contributors than spending millions on consultants could deliver!

In September, when he gets behind his new desk as the BBC's 17th Director-General, Tim Davie faces more than one crisis.

The knives are still out in government; the issue of over-75s' licence fees; the decriminalisation of non-payment of the licence fee; major talent slugging it out over the gender pay gap; the parliamentary review of the funding of the BBC; and the continuous and very public job reduction proposals and cost cutting to address financial challenges.

Take a breath. There are more...

The rise of on-demand viewing; the increase in eGaming options; technological change; social media battles; fear-of-missing-out (FOMO) influencers; perceptions of bias; dramatic increase in globalised competition; and an anti-BBC press.

While the Covid-19 crisis may have seen these issues fall away from the headlines, the cogs still turn behind the scenes. When government need a diversion from its own woes, expect the BBC to be again one of the targets in the months ahead.

These issues are in some ways sideshows to the single biggest challenge that underpins universal public service media (PSM) – and that is actually having an audience to watch, to listen, to browse, to consume. Mark Damazer, former controller of BBC Radio 4, former BBC Trustee and now an expert former BBC insider called it "…the single most important thing that has to be gripped, but it's not easy".

Throughout the book we have deliberately tried to get views from across the whole of the UK, from different generations and from different backgrounds. As a result there is, of course, no consensus in what the BBC needs to do to win the young audience. There are however some themes emerging.

On-demand or no demand…

Very little content is now demanded live by the audience – perhaps only news and sport. These events bring families and communities into shared viewing experiences. It will be interesting over the summer, when more free live sport is on the BBC than has been in recent years, to see how big the audience will be.

All other content can be on-demand for the younger audience – which should make the BBC's job easier. So why make it harder by debating the return of BBC Three as a linear channel?

In the short term there will be a lack of original high quality content due to the pause in production during the pandemic. Studios are simply not making output.

So, for a time, repeats and archive content will fill all schedules of linear services to a degree not usually seen. This will drive the audience back to on-demand, an audience which has been using linear while in lockdown. And the return may take longer to get back to normal than expected as talent, both on and behind the camera, is in short supply and projects will be backed up. Expect it to be the end of 2021 before this plays out in its entirety.

Young audiences are unforgiving and will find content to engage them. The BBC needs to publish its programming plan for post-Covid that is just as engaging and dynamic and broad as its output through the crisis.

The tech needs to be good

The audience is leading this change but that audience wants to watch more than BBC content. The BBC has to decide how material is shared with other platform providers so it sits side by side with competitors' programming. Or being even more radical – how much material by other providers can sit inside the BBC environment? The Britbox partnership with ITV is perhaps the start of this.

The BBC technologists should be left to (re)invent new distribution products. When the iPlayer was launched it was world leading. Make the BBC's technology interoperable, allow it to sit easily in competition environments. Inflexibility is not a good look.

Can BBC technology find a way to deliver a BBC app with iPlayer and social media streaming – for good and bad – that can be used in smart TV apps, in other platforms and set top boxes and as a stand-alone OTT offering? This would truly engage the multi-screen young audience in its and others content. Make it shareable, accessible and sociable. Ed Vaizey described it as being an 'open platform', not a closed one.

Positive regulatory intervention

Much of the future of the BBC lies outside its own control: the regulator and the Government through primary legislation have to ensure that PSM content is at the forefront of all distribution platforms in the UK.

So often PSM programming doesn't have the prominence it does on linear television. Ofcom has consulted on this and sees the importance, but really the Government has to act too through legislation.

That single issue must be resolved for a time when all media is consumed on demand and digitally and linear channels are merely shopfronts for their VOD collections.

And while the EU and the latest iteration of its Audio-Visual Media Services Directive aim to level the regulatory playing field between public service and social media television-like content, there has to be a realisation at some point in both the Government and Ofcom that all content has to be regulated equally. That is only harm and offence and balance should be regulated along with protection of children.

There is real regard for the quality of BBC content, but it's on a programme-by-programme, talent-by-talent, piece-by piece-basis.

The BBC could help itself by 'minding the gap'. CBeebies caters for under six year olds, CBBC from six-12 and then BBC Three is aimed at 16-34s. Those early teenage years are formative in many ways, including media consumption habits, so the BBC needs to urgently address this lack of service to the 12-16-year-old audience to become part of young viewers' and listeners' habits.

The young audience cares much less about brand and much more about engagement. Young people do want water-cooler content. They may not watch it together (when was the last time you sat around the television as a family or in a group and watched the same thing at the same time?) but they do want to share the experience and talk about it online and on social media.

Some of this can come from the BBC, still loved by young people when shared on YouTube. The BBC should be packaging the 'gold' for the next generation – short form, compilations, outtakes – all shareable.

Interestingly, the BBC-owned UKTV says demand in the lockdown among 18-30-year-olds for programmes like *Birds of a Feather*, classic *EastEnders* and *Casualty* was high and the top ten of its linear shows included *Only Fools and Horses* and *The Vicar of Dibley*.

This could be a perfect time to raid the archive, when schedules are weak because of the Covid production hiatus. Some imaginative thought would lead to a quick win.

The more places the BBC touches the audience, the warmer they will feel. The BBC needs to create TV and radio that's not TV and radio – but platform neutral, tech neutral and audience positive.

An appetite for risk needs to be nurtured: talent, production, subject matter all come into this. Be like Channel 4 in its glory days. Edgy, sometimes challenging boundaries, but talked about for the right reasons.

Paul Robinson talked about the loss of the Radio 1 roadshow – how it entertained hundreds of thousands in person and millions more on the radio each summer.

Can the BBC reinvent itself to be closer to the audience? *Proms in the Park* and the *Big Weekend* are single fireworks – how can the BBC fill the sky with colour?

The licence fee is now £157.50, that's about 0.43p a day, around £3 a week. The BBC used to call itself 'the best bargain in Britain' and perhaps it still is.

Now any marketeer will tell you why that slogan was dropped – a high-quality provider of PSM does not want to be seen in the 'bargain bucket'. However any good marketeer should also been able to promote the breadth of the BBC offering and the 'value' rather than the 'price'.

The BBC has failed to blow its own trumpet. Yes it promotes the programming, but it needs to promote the institution too. Not in a brash, commercial way but in a cultural, educational, diverse and inclusive role.

One of the best ever media releases I have seen from the BBC was the huge change in the corporation's output and focus on programming when the Covid-19 crisis hit.

The clock is ticking on the licence fee

Streamlining programming, focusing on education and inclusion and prioritising core-news. It can move fast and effectively when it has focus and purpose of mission. I suspect the changes made by the BBC during the crisis never touched a focus group or market research – and look at the results, almost universal success in terms of audience appreciation.

But undoubtedly a countdown is taking place. Recent reports into the funding of the BBC have continued to support the licence fee, indeed it may be the best way to fund an organisation as unique as the BBC but the support of the young audience for that mechanism has almost totally evaporated. While the BBC will hold on and fight as long as possible, plan B will be needed at some point.

The BBC may have to give a little on the size of the licence fee to ensure it continues as a payment mechanism for some time to come. Perhaps a lower flat fee a year for the linear BBC services (remember there is no technology that allows subscription for terrestrial television or radio) but BBC iPlayer and BBC Sounds could come with a stand-alone subscription fee.

The young audience appear happy to pay for services they use and the digital, on-demand services can be metered.

Other countries are looking at different payment models for PSM. Ireland has discussed a communications charge, basically additional direct taxation. Switzerland has reduced dramatically its licence fee and, in the USA, PSMs are funded by telethons, radiothons and advertising.

Maybe the licence fee makes the BBC strong, but some are arguing it's the very mechanism that stops reform.

Make it modern

Few of the younger audience see the BBC as a business, but its competitors do. And they create the headlines and stories that knock the BBC for, among many things, its inefficiency.

Those who work in the commercial sector can see it a mile off. I once had a boozy dinner with a senior (as in very senior) BBC executive, and they admitted that anyone with commercial experience could take 25 per cent of BBC costs out of the system with very little effect on programming.

I disagreed – it's closer to a third, I said.

The management structures, the internal services that could be outsourced; the fiefdoms could all be swept away; and many workflows can be modernised. Decentralise from highly expensive central London locations to across the UK and be far more reflective of the audience.

Many of the young people spoken to when researching the book viewed the BBC as irrelevant. That has to change – representation is improving, but portrayal and realism are key. Farrukh Dhondy says it may mean more sex and violence from Auntie, but *Peaky Binders* and *Normal People* have found a way to balance brilliance with blushes and brutality.

Make simple great, unique public service media

Under represented backgrounds should not be shoehorned into content, either in scripted or unscripted programming. They need to be integrated to really resonate with the audience.

It needs to inform, to entertain and to educate not just the young audience, but all audiences. But it cannot inhabit the same space as other broadcasters – it needs to be more. It must be less inward looking and understand its part in the ecosystem. It must ensure it's in as many parts of that ecosystem as possible, and reflect the real country at large. End the 'modern, urban outlook' as the current Culture Secretary put it.

With the ITV regional licences being up for renewal in 2024, there is a likelihood it will try to reduce regional commitments event further. The BBC will be the only show in many towns. Instead of the recently announced reductions in regional programming, the BBC should be making content on both radio and television that reflects the regional and nations as a core part of its output. The closer the audience feels to the BBC the more loyal the audience should become.

The Covid crisis made news accessible. Lockdown meant guests contributed from their own front room and viewers' video and social media content was used in every report. Audiences increased. As we return to more normal conditions, there is more traditionally gathered interviews and pictures and as a result TV news feels like it has regressed and become old fashioned again.

Audience-sourced content, while requiring verification, makes stories much more real to a young audience. It also allows broadcasters to have cameras across the entire country; places and communities were represented during Covid that often don't get a look in at other times.

Time and time again the BBC's desire to appear unbiased has the opposite effect. There are some stories where there isn't another side. There are some stories that simply need to be called out as lies or false. There are some personal views that speak for themselves. Ofcom asks for due impartiality. It is not the same as impartiality – a little more emphasis on the due would go a long way.

A redefined public service media will not be a monolith, but a layered, effective partner. The BBC partners now brilliantly with the arts, but it needs to do more with the technology platforms.

The BBC gets credit for *Normal People*. That was a partnership with Hulu and Screen Ireland. *Fleabag* was a partnership with Amazon Studios.

How can these partnerships be extended to bring the talent and the content to a wide audience? Can the BBC forge an even stronger relationship with other global PSM producers; more co-productions, help share budgets and nurturing new talent to compete with the likes of Amazon, Netflix and Apple.

When commissioning content for the new generation and building a new definition of PSM the BBC needs to ask itself: "How is this part of our DNA?" If that question cannot be clearly answered then the project should not be commissioned. The young audience – all audiences – want to know what the BBC offering is. Its reach and its breadth, not necessarily its scale.

My son is three years old. He doesn't understand why the edition of his favourite children's programme isn't the one he loves, rather than the one the scheduler puts out. He is used to getting the programmes he wants to see on demand. He won't watch advertising and he's happy scrolling through YouTube Kids to be entertained.

He is the next generation who won't want anything served up by schedulers. He will want to self-select and navigate by recommendation (both from friends and from cross-promotion), algorithm and instinct.

This is the place the BBC needs to inhabit – to jump 20 years ahead and reinvent public service media.

The biggest set of challenges for any DG to inherit

The world has moved on. When a teenager making a vlog in their bedroom can get millions of views on YouTube without a broadcaster or a production company then the positioning of the BBC needs some redefinition.

Twenty years ago, the then DG John Birt made some impressive decisions to future proof the BBC, but through crisis after crisis since then the BBC has been short term in its strategy. A long-term vision is required...urgently.

There is no doubt that the BBC is still the most used media organisation in the UK. In the linear and on-demand TV world, time with the BBC is estimated to be around 31 per cent compared to around nine per cent for Netflix.

The BBC is needed more than ever in the 21st century in an age of disinformation. And there are plenty of reasons. 'Fake news'; political lies pedalled as fact; globalisation of content; helping to define a post-Brexit United Kingdom to both a home and international audience; contextualising social media outrage; and being a cultural institution not motivated by short-term commercial returns.

These pages do not, deliberately, lay out a road map or a menu for the BBC to attract young people. The BBC is a complex organisation and a tweak here can create a tsunami over there.

However, new DG Tim Davie knows that more than a tweak is needed. Root and branch reform is required in the organisation, which is already hugely demoralised internally by constant changes and external advice. Plus it has a traditional core audience that doesn't like change, loves its familiar programmes and talent, and may not be wed to new technology.

Even the BBC's own media editor said on the BBC *News at Ten* in June when Davie was announced as DG that he faces the biggest set of challenges in his inbox of any incoming editor-in-chief of the organisation.

There are sideshows – many of them important to address – but for Tim Davie to succeed at DG and to regain a funding settlement and Royal Charter that will continue to deliver an innovative and bold BBC in 2027 he must reinvent strong, characterful public service media attractive to the whole of the UK and beyond by engaging all audiences, and especially the young.

As Dr Victoria McCollum succinctly puts it, to attract the young audience the BBC needs to not just 'inform, educate and entertain', but it must also 'enlighten, challenge and involve'.

Chapter 21

What they really think: a final view from the target audience

In attracting a younger audience, Rebecca Beavington – one of those being chased – says the BBC is doing pretty well, but it needs to up its game to avoid losing too much to its rivals. Can it do it?

The nature of how people consume media has changed drastically over the last decade with the rise of streaming services, podcasts and social media.

In a rapidly evolving media landscape, the BBC has also been evolving and adapting. It has always had a central role in news consumption both in the UK and with its international reach – and I think it will always have a part to play. But the question is what sort of role? Will it be able to adapt fast enough amid the current pace of change?

If the BBC is losing listeners, it might want to consider targeting its stations at a younger audience, making the content more relatable to a younger demographic.

The BBC has an established role in audiences' general media use and I don't think that will ever change. However, with the launch of the BBC Sounds app in 2018, I feel that it has attracted a much wider base among the younger generation.

The app allows both live listening and on-demand radio, which is very convenient for my generation as we are all constantly on the move and busy doing things. And as a BBC radio fan I now know I can go to the app and listen to one of my favourites presenters wherever I want – as long as I have an internet connection. My impression is that the launch of BBC Sounds has helped the BBC retain its listeners because they can now listen on their phones.

Of course, the BBC is not the only ones doing this. But the BBC has improved massively in its attempts to engage younger audiences with its radio stations (Radio1 and 1Xtra especially). I say this because the two have well-deserved reputations for creativity and innovation. With a range of inspirational presenters that all have such big, unique personalities they seem to all deliver the content and music that we as a younger audience are drawn to and enjoy.

I follow 1Xtra on social media accounts and I feel that it is great at constantly keeping up to date with its audience and delivering us really good content daily. And I do feel that 1Xtra is more relatable to younger audiences rather than Radio 1 and has more listeners in its target grouping.

The BBC Sounds app also gives listeners access to a range of podcasts, which is something that has become a massive trend in recent years – a trend that has quickened over the last year especially.

One of the major benefits of podcasts is that you can listen to them whenever you want and save episodes up for a long journey. But you can also listen to them the moment they're released. If you have to stop a podcast halfway through, you can simply pick it up again where you left off or go back to the beginning and start again.

It is great that the BBC is releasing its own unique podcasts and – don't get me wrong – there is absolutely nothing wrong with its podcasts. But the issue facing the BBC is that it is just one of many streaming services providing podcasts.

Spotify has a very wide range of podcasts, as does iTunes, Apple and many more. I could search in 'podcasts on positivity' on Spotify and hundreds of episodes would come up from different podcast creators/hosts all over the world. But for the BBC this isn't the same, and this is one of the issues to why it is losing its younger audiences.

In the end I think that the BBC has had to adapt to a rapidly changing media landscape. For audio programs, broadcast radio has some stiff competition from podcasts and streaming services. While the BBC has adapted well with its Sounds app, competition from Spotify and others is likely to see it lose more of its audience. In terms of the younger audience, it is doing well, but it needs to up its game and make sure it remains relevant.

The BBC will always be a part of the audio media offering, but it remains to be seen just how big a part of this it will be in the future.

About the writer

Rebecca Beavington has just graduated from The Global Academy in Hayes. She has always wanted to go into the media industry and broadcasting in particular. Radio presenting is a passion of Rebecca's and she recently entered the Young Audio Awards and won the award for BBC Rising Talent and from this wishes to continue on her journey, taking her passion for presenting further.

Bite-Sized Public Affairs Books are designed to provide insights and stimulating ideas that affect us all in, for example, journalism, social policy, education, government and politics.

They are deliberately short, easy to read, and authoritative books written by people who are either on the front line or who are informed observers. They are designed to stimulate discussion, thought and innovation in all areas of public affairs. They are all firmly based on personal experience and direct involvement and engagement.

The most successful people all share an ability to focus on what really matters, keeping things simple and understandable. When we are faced with a new challenge most of us need quick guidance on what matters most, from people who have been there before and who can show us where to start.

They can be read straight through at one easy sitting and then referred to as necessary – a trusted repository of hard-won experience.

Bite-Sized Books Catalogue

We publish Business Books, Life-Style Books, Public Affairs Books, including our Brexit Books, Fiction – both short form and long form – and Children's Fiction.

To see our full range of books, please go to https://bite-sizedbooks.com/.

Printed in Great Britain
by Amazon